Coaching Tools

Coaching Tools

A further 123 coaching tools and techniques for executive coaches, team coaches, mentors and supervisors: Volume 3

Edited by

Jonathan Passmore, Claudia Day, Julie Flower,

Maggie Grieve and Jelena Jovanovic Moon

First published in 2023 by Libri Publishing

Copyright © Libri Publishing

The right of Jonathan Passmore, Claudia Day, Julie Flower, Maggie Grieve and Jelena Jovanovic Moon to be identified as the editors of this work has been asserted in accordance with the Copyright, Designs and Patents Act, 1988.

ISBN 978-1-911450-90-0

A CIP catalogue record for this book is available from The British Library

Cover and Design by Carnegie Book Production
Cover graphic by Mina Krstajic

Printed in the UK by Halstan

Libri Publishing
Brunel House
Volunteer Way
Faringdon
Oxfordshire
SN7 7YR

Tel: +44 (0)845 873 3837

www.libripublishing.co.uk

Contents

Contributors

Badri Bajaj

Magdalena Bak-Maier

Emily Barber

Clodagh Beaty

Michael Bungay Stanier

Julia Carden

Layla Coe

Sarah Corrie

Elaine Cox

Dave Crome

Elizabeth Crosse

Claudia Day

Jonathan Drew

Anthony
Eldridge-Rogers

Claire Finch

Julie Flower

Bob Garvey

Andrew George

Andrea Giraldez-Hayes

Jackie Gittins

Sarah Gledhill

Marshall Goldsmith

Maggie Grieve

Karen Hayns

Derek Hill

Eileen Hutchinson

Marc Innegraeve

Sam Isaacson

Ann James

Whitney Johnson

Jelena Jovanovic Moon

Francesca King

David A. Lane

Paul Lawrence

Hayley Lewis

Christine Lithgow Smith

David Love

Michelle Lucas

Mongezi C. Makhalima

Darko Markovic

Deb McEwen

Haesun Moon

Felix Müller

Rosie Nice

Clare Norman

Joe Oliver

Callum O'Neill

Francoise Orlov

Jonathan Passmore

Theresa Quinn

Claire Rason

Manfusa Shams

Phil Summerfield

Catherine Wilton

Woody Woodward

Cathleen Wu

The Editors

Jonathan Passmore

Jonathan is a respected international thought leader in coaching. He is senior vice president at EZRA, LHH, and professor of coaching and behavioural change, Henley Business School. Prior to this he has worked for PWC, IBM Business Consulting and CoachHub in a range of leadership roles. He is an accredited executive coach, supervisor and chartered psychologist. He has published widely, producing 40 books on coaching, leadership, change and mindfulness, including *Becoming a Coach: The Essential ICF Guide* and *The Coaches' Handbook*, and over 250 scientific papers and book chapters. His work has been recognised with multiple awards from professional bodies including the British Psychological Society, the Association of Business Psychologists and the EMCC.

Jonathan Passmore

Maggie Grieve

Maggie is a leadership and team coach with 30 years of board-level strategy, partnering and business development experience. She left her global partnering strategy director role with BT Plc in 2016 to start Ping Thinking, where she pursues her combined passions of people and strategy by helping businesses, teams and individuals create meaningful, structured and supported change, with an emphasis on recognition, appreciation and utilisation of their own strengths and resources. Maggie holds professional qualifications in executive (Henley) and team (WBECS) coaching, a business degree (BA) and marketing diploma (CIM) and is an accredited EMCC team coach, AC professional coach and Lumina psychometrics practitioner.

Maggie Grieve

Julie Flower

Julie Flower is a leadership development consultant, facilitator and coach who focuses on positive social change impact in complex systems. She holds an MSc in coaching and behavioural change and is an external tutor in executive coaching at Henley Business School. With senior experience in the public, private and non-profit sectors, Julie leads The Specialist Generalist, a learning and development practice. She is also an international and award-winning improvised-comedy performer who integrates learning from improv with other evidence-based behavioural change approaches to help leaders and teams navigate uncertainty.

Julie Flower

Claudia Day

Claudia is a back-to-work coach, who after starting her family and working in multiple roles and industries across the globe – including cancer research, management consulting, NGOs and customer retention – appreciated how difficult change can be. This motivated her to venture into the industry. Claudia holds professional qualifications in executive coaching from Henley Business School, an MBA from MIT Sloan School of Management and is accredited by EMCC. She is also an entrepreneur and a co-founder of My Coaching Place, an online coaching platform designed to provide coaches with an end-to-end solution that covers admin, development and remote coaching.

Claudia Day

Jelena Jovanovic Moon

Jelena is a psychologist with degrees in coaching and organisational change from Henley Business School and people management from LSE. Holding senior leadership and consulting roles in people management and organisational development across the private, public and non-profit sectors, she has supported organisations through fast growth and people in embracing change. This is where she discovered her passion for coaching, as any successful change starts with a lightbulb moment in someone's mind. Now, through coaching, she is driven to switch on as many lightbulbs as possible.

Jelena Jovanovic Moon

Acknowledgements

We would like to thank the Libri team for their support in what started as one book and has now turned out to be a three-volume project. In particular, Celia and John who have remained constant with us at the heart of this adventure – it's always a delight working with them.

We would also like to thank colleagues at Henley Business School and our respective families for their understanding, as much of the work for books such as this happens outside of the day job when we might otherwise be engaging in family time.

The combined books, packed with generously shared, diversely achieved, knowledge and expertise, collated through this highly ambitious project, would be nothing without the freely given time and experience of our 121 contributors. The books are a labour of real love, and we have a sense of enormous achievement, on everyone's behalf, of sharing the very best in coaching worldwide.

Introduction

"Individually, we are one drop. Together, we are an ocean."

Ryunosuke Satoro

Something amazing happens when people invest and work towards the same goal – things change. Our Coaching Tools books – a collaborative effort, that draws together coaches from around the world to share their favourite practices – are living evidence of that. The result is, we hope, the richest collection of coaching tools and techniques ever compiled, providing coaching professionals with a wonderful resource.

Before you read Volume 3, perhaps you'd like to hear a little about the background of why we created the books and how they are different from any other coaching books. For a group of experienced coaches and business leaders, enrolled on the Coaching and Behavioural Change MSc at Henley Business School, the pressure was on. A submission deadline loomed, and supportive advice and encouragement flowed in ever-increasing quantities between group members. A seemingly innocent question suddenly stopped us all dead in our tracks: "Can anyone recommend a good coaching techniques and tools book?" A simple question for a group awash with coaching experience. Surely a river of suggestions would instantly flow. But what happened was a moment's silence, as we all stopped to think. Of course, after a while, some suggestions emerged, but what remained was a realisation that despite our tremendous combined experience, none of us had a 'best' coaching book that we could suggest for capable, professional coaches to turn to, for a wide variety of evidence-based coaching tools and techniques. The question lingered and caused the group to consider how we might change this. Four of us volunteered to champion the idea and before too long, we garnered support from our Henley professor, Jonathan Passmore, who also saw the potential.

Together, we embarked on exploring and developing the idea further.

Thoughts emerged on how a resource like this, with tried-and-tested methodology at its heart, provided in a highly visual, easy-to-read, inviting-to-browse-through-and-reflect-on format, could really help coaches to prepare for exceptional client sessions. We reached out across the Henley network and collected a large handful of coaches' great favourites. Our initial aim was for 50, but enthusiasm and momentum increased as our 'best of the best' concept gained visibility in the wider professional coaching community and, before we knew it, our 50 had become over 200. The project, now known as *WeCoach!*, continued to expand, and with it came enthusiastic contributions from those at the very top of our field: exciting! Something very special and new had been created – a full and wholesome collection of favourite tools from an exceptional group of coaches, ready to be shared with the worldwide coaching community.

Our excitement and achievement gained the attention of our proposed publishers and now our idea looked like it could become a reality. This story is at the very heart of the volume you now hold in your hands – a collaboration and contribution of tried-and-tested personal favourites from amongst the very best in our field, provided as an easy-to-use, rich source of applied tools and techniques that had hitherto not existed. All of this could never have been achieved without the valuable contributions and support of 120 plus fellow coaches who helped create these books, and for this we thank them all. It is this that changed our single drop of an idea into an ocean of joint achievement.

During the process, we decided to make the books stand out from anything that had been produced before. First for the diversity and the scale of contributions and contributors to create an acknowledged go-to resource with more than 200 tools and two volumes. This has now been expanded to three volumes, with well over 300 tools in total.

Second for the eclectic nature of the tools, reflecting the range of contributors, drawing disparately from Behavioural, Cognitive Behavioural, Motivational Interviewing, Acceptance and Commitment Therapy, Compassion, Positive Psychology, Psychodynamic, Gestalt, Solution-focused, Mindfulness and Neuroscience frameworks, amongst others.

Third, inspired by the idea of the accessibility and usefulness of a really good recipe book, we decided to present the books in an easy-to-use design with each tool easy to find, containing clear ingredients, a description and a step-by-step method. Of course, coaching is not cooking. The coach needs to decide which, if any, tool to use with a client, and how to introduce it. Whilst the presentation is common across the tools and simple in its structure, we hope that coaches will add them to their repertoire and adapt them in unique ways to ensure each client is respected for the unique and wonderful creation they are.

The final ambition, which struck fear into many of the publishers we approached, was our decision to publish the books in colour, rich with images to inspire coaches in their work – useful and beautiful in equal measure. Thankfully, our publisher, Libri, also understood how all these elements combined to provide something with great potential for professional coaches and so, the collection and the presentation became a reality.

Turning our idea into books has absolutely been as hard as it sounds, but the reward of creating a resource that supports the global coach community to help leaders, managers and people all over the world has made every minute of effort worthwhile. So, the next time someone blithely asks the question "can anyone recommend…" we hope there will be no silence and you will offer them our Coaching Tools books as the very best resource of coaching tools, methods and techniques, knowledge and wisdom available.

Welcome to Volume 3!

What Is a Coaching Tool?

During coach training and as you progress through your career, you are likely to draw on a range of theoretical approaches and pick up a sometimes-dizzying array of tools and techniques. It may seem that each new development module or learning workshop you attend presents yet more handy diagrams, acronyms and models. As coaches, we believe in an evidence-based but diverse approach, which includes tools, techniques, models and exercises that experienced contributors have found useful in their coaching work with clients.

Tools, by definition, are helpful when focused on a particular job. The skill of the coach is to identify when one of these may be useful, to support a client with a particular situation, issue or aim. The tools are drawn from a range of different coaching approaches (such as cognitive behavioural, humanistic and Gestalt) and other disciplines as diverse as leadership and management theory and improvised comedy. They include questioning techniques, visual models, practical frameworks and some very creative approaches. All can help to bring structure and focus to your coaching conversations. We hope that they will provide inspiration and food for thought, and find practical application in your work.

They are intended to be used, adapted and integrated into your wider coaching practice, within the bounds of your own professional competence, preference and curiosity. You will amplify the use of the tools through the quality of your questions, your presence and your knowledge of underpinning coaching theory and the evidence around behavioural change. They are presented in an easy-to-follow 'recipe' format but are not intended to bring a formulaic approach to coaching. Many of the tools can be used equally well in individual and group or team coaching settings. It is hoped that you will find something in here to add to your existing repertoire of tools and techniques, in order to best support your clients.

A tool is only a tool and can never replace a strong client relationship, a sound theoretical base or core coaching skills. Both Hardingham (2006) and Passmore (2007) advocate an 'eclectic' approach that synthesises tools, techniques and frameworks from a range of approaches through their respective British Eclectic and Integrated Coaching models. The emphasis remains on the client, the relationship and the context. However, coaching tools can provide clients with new and helpful ways of exploring situations, reflecting and structuring their thoughts, as well as gaining commitment to act. They can also provide a refreshing change in energy and different way of working, for both client and coach.

References

Hardingham, A. (2006) The British Eclectic Model of Coaching: Towards Professionalism without Dogma. *International Journal of Mentoring and Coaching*, IV(1): 11–14.

Passmore, J. (2007) An Integrated Model for Executive Coaching. *Consulting Psychology Journal*, 59(1): 68–78.

How to Introduce Tools to Clients

In deciding which tool to use, coaches should follow their experience and wisdom (Wilson, 2014, p.222). As an integrated coach drawing on a range of models, your focus will be to select a tool based on your client and their presenting issue, whilst also taking into account your own training and strengths (Passmore, 2021).

As coaches, we know that potential tools have to help clients to move on when stuck, to develop fresh thinking or to create new insights. But for the client, any tool we offer is likely to be new to them. Some clients may have had negative experiences with something similar, for example being told that they cannot draw. This can lead to a reluctance to step out of their comfort zone or traditional ways of working, for example if invited to play with Lego or go for a coaching walk.

It is important to keep in mind the following risks when introducing a tool:
- The client might not like the tool or may feel uncomfortable with it.
- The client might not engage with the tool – for instance, if they feel fear that it might reveal something they are not ready to handle, or because they have no faith in it being effective.
- The tool may not have the impact the coach expects, and it may not move the client forward or generate new awareness.
- It might break rapport.
- The tool may challenge the skills of the client.
- The tool may be difficult to execute with the resources available (e.g. physical space).
- The tool may be subjected to perceptions that the client holds of how things are and should be.

Taking into consideration all of the above, when introducing a tool, the coach needs to make sure they do it in a way that avoids these risks.

Eight guiding principles

1. **Choice**: Choose the tool based on the client's needs and not your personal agenda.
2. **Rapport**: Make sure rapport is strong. If rapport is broken at the early stages of the relationship, it may be more difficult to build it again than if there is a strong relationship already (Hardingham, 2004).
3. **Time**: Be aware how long you have in the session. Some tools can be introduced without any explanation, some are short, maybe less than a minute, while others may take the whole coaching session.
4. **Consent**: Ask for permission: "Would you be comfortable if we did something a little different?"
5. **Explain**: Give background about the tool, an overview of how it has been used in the past and how it could be helpful in this case.
6. **Options**: Give the client options. The driver of the coaching relationship is the client: they always have the option to give the tool a try – or not.
7. **Experiment**: Explain that it is an 'experiment' – and just see how it goes. This gives you and them the right for the experiment to 'fail', with no pressure or expectation on either side.
8. **Reflect**: Reflect on how it went, both with the client and on your own, to learn from the experience and use it in future sessions.

While tools can add to our work with clients, they need to be introduced sensitively and tactfully, respecting each individual and the issues they bring.

References

Hardingham, A. (2004) *The Coach's Coach*. London: Chartered Institute of Personnel and Development.

Passmore, J. (2021) Developing an Integrated Coaching Approach. In J. Passmore (ed.), *The Coaches' Handbook: The Complete Practitioner Guide for Professional Coaches*, pp.322–330. Abingdon: Routledge.

Wilson, C. (2014) *Performance Coaching: A Complete Guide to Best Practice Coaching and Training* (2nd edition). London: Kogan Page.

The Four 'I's

Ingredients

None

Description

An effective and simple technique to help the client to summarise and organise their thinking towards the end of a coaching conversation. Described by Lancer, Clutterbuck and Megginson (2016), the Four 'I's are:

Issues – what was discussed?

Ideas – what interesting concepts were surfaced?

Insights – what new awareness came to light?

Intentions – what actions will the client take following the conversation?

When does it work best?

The Four 'I's are effective in most coaching conversations. They may be particularly useful for a client who asks for advice from the coach, as a way to draw out the client's thinking. They can also be helpful when the conversation has taken various paths, as a way to help the client bring a number of disparate strands together.

Step by step

1. Towards the end of the session, as it reaches a break, say "It seems that we have come to a natural pause" and wait for the client to agree or continue thinking.
2. Ask "What key **issues** have we discussed today?" Allow the client to reflect and articulate what they feel have been the key issues. These can be different from those noted by the coach, which further validates the importance of the client summarising their own issues.
3. Once the client has finished summarising the key issues, next ask "What interesting **ideas** have come up?" This question can also elicit new ideas or a reframing of those that were discussed.
4. Then ask "What **insights** have you had during our conversation?" Allow the client to fully express their insights.
5. Finally, ask "And what **intentions** do you have as a result of this discussion?"
6. You may ask questions that aid the client to clarify their intentions and to support them to develop specific actions. Alternatively, you may ask scaling or similar questions to determine the client's level of motivation and commitment towards these new intentions.

Reference

Lancer, N., Clutterbuck, D., and Megginson, D. (2016) *Techniques for Coaching and Mentoring* (2nd edition). Abingdon: Routledge.

Sarah Gledhill is an accredited coach who specialises in the higher education and non-profit sectors, following an international fundraising career.

Developmental Mindset Inventory (DMI)

Ingredients

Paper and pens

When does it work best?

The DMI inventory can be used to identify and regularly review your developmental needs and learning requirements. This helps create a dynamic, continuous personal and professional development plan that evolves to meet your emerging needs. It can also help as a cost–benefit analysis when you are considering a significant investment in a developmental opportunity.

Description

The Developmental Mindset Inventory (DMI), Figure 1, is an evidenced-based tool that can be used for a more comprehensive approach to planning continuous coach development. Its purpose is to encourage you to think holistically when exploring 'what's next' for your learning journey. It asks you to consider your coaching purpose and personal requirements as well as your developmental focus. There is no 'right' way to work with the DMI. Use your criteria for making judgements, so this tool works for you. Your aim is to create a practical development plan that feels inspiring and addresses the unique and contextual nature of your development needs.

Step by step

1. **Identify your coaching purpose:** What is the scope of your purpose? How do you want your coaching to make a difference? Is this about direct benefit for the individual client or are you looking to have a broader impact at an organisational or societal level? You may even be looking to contribute to the profession.
2. **Define each area:** Generic descriptors have been given in the table below, but creating your definition means you can interpret the concept in a relevant way.

Developmental focus	Personal requirements
The Art of Coaching: what is needed to develop the depth and complexity with which you can notice, operate and change?	Business needs: relevance for mainlining a commercial coaching practice.
The Being of Coaching: What is needed to develop reflective practice and work authentically?	Learning needs: learning styles, methods of delivery, the format of the programme and assessment (if relevant).
The Craft of Coaching: What knowledge and skills are needed for professional practice?	Practical needs: cost, travel, commitment.

3. **Assess each area:** Use the questions in the grid below to help you assess how important each area is to you now. Then consider each area in turn. Use a scale of 0–10 (where 0 is low, 10 is high) to reflect how important each area feels to you and create your 'wheel' on the DMI.

Developmental Mindset Inventory (DMI)

The questions

	When thinking about my development needs, how important is it for me to consider each of the following?		
The Art of Coaching:	• Opportunities to contribute to the coaching profession • My capability to support other coaches' development • Opportunities for meaningful connections with other coaches • Doing coaching research • Learning from coaching research	Business needs:	• Feedback for clients • How I can differentiate myself from other coaches • Gaining a qualification/ credential required by clients • If it will help grow my coaching business • Enhancing my reputation as a coach
The Being of Coaching:	• Participating in formal supervision • Doing some deep self-work (maybe therapy) • Enhancing my general wellbeing • Broadening my understanding of world issues • My commitment to diversity and inclusion	Learning needs:	• Refreshing my existing skills and knowledge • Having an intellectual challenge • Engaging in experiential (activity-based) learning • Feedback on my coaching from more experienced coaches • Being pushed out of my comfort zone
The Craft of Coaching:	• Something to boost my confidence • Being assessed against a competency-based framework • Gaining expertise in a particular genre of coaching • Non-coaching learning, e.g. psychometric training • Getting new tools and techniques	Practical needs:	• The cost • What will be recognised as CPD by my professional coaching body? • The credibility of the provider • Alignment with a specific development strategy • What else is going on in my life

4. **Some further questions:** When thinking about my development needs, how important is it for me to consider each of the following?
   • The values and beliefs that underpin my coaching
   • Enhancing my ethical maturity
   • The way I develop authentic coaching relationships
   • Getting better at critical thinking
   • My own resilience

5. **Take action:** Use your insights from this exercise and think about the next steps for your development.
   - What do you want to commit to?
   - What resources/challenges do you need to consider?
   - How will you monitor and review?

Figure 1: Developmental Mindset

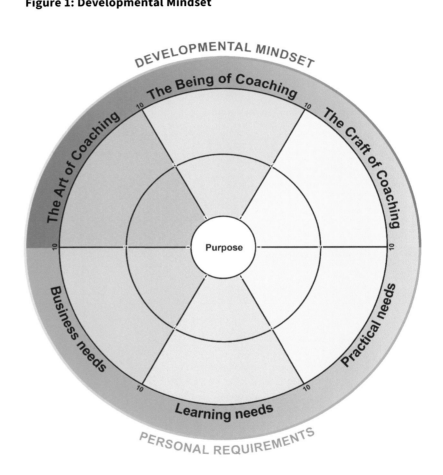

Reference

Crosse, E. (2023) A Q Methodology Study. A Journey of Expertise: How Executive Coaches Identify Their Development Needs. Unpublished doctoral thesis. Oxford Brookes University.

Note: Diagrams are reproduced with the agreement of Elizabeth Crosse.

Elizabeth Crosse is an ICF MCC mentor coach and supervisor. Her research and practice focus on coaches' continuous professional and personal development.

Team Coaching with the Dialogic Orientation Quadrant (DOQ)

Ingredients

Masking Tape
Flipcharts/something to write or post on
Pen
Sticky Notes

When does it work best?

This exercise will work best when the group size is larger than 12. For a smaller team, it might be useful to invite the conversation in each quadrant in the sequence 3, 4, 1, 2. This exercise may be useful for new teams or experienced teams in different ways. It will be particularly useful if hearing from different perspectives is important. This may not be the most effective tool for decision-making but it will be highly effective as a collective meaning-making tool for teams to experience.

Description

Working in and with teams often offers unique opportunities to consider multiple perspectives and expertise, yet it may pose a relational challenge when the team members may not have a coherent shared meaning of their desired directions, preferred possibilities or sense of progress. This simple activity creates dialogic conditions for team members to converse in a safe and appreciative manner with one another, so that it engages people to have more conversations and have them better. This activity is based on an heuristic of interaction used in coaching research called the Dialogic Orientation Quadrant (DOQ). This offers two intersecting continuums of timeline and preference in narratives. There are four quadrants (sections) in the model, as shown in the diagram.

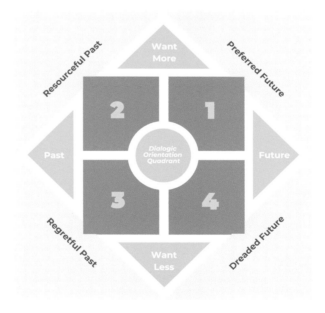

- Quadrant 1 (Upper-right): Preferred Future
- Quadrant 2 (Upper-left): Resourceful Past
- Quadrant 3 (Bottom-left): Troubled Past
- Quadrant 4 (Bottom-right): Dreaded Future

This exercise invites participants to engage in each of the quadrants in an appreciative and reflective way with one another, often resulting in curating collective and collaborative stories of purpose, possibilities and progress.

Step by step

1. Section off a room into four areas (quadrants) using masking tape or other indicating objects or barriers.
2. Give a quick orientation about the DOQ (both the concept and the floor layout) to the participating team members.
3. Set up a flipchart in each section of the quadrant labelled as above, starting from the upper-right corner and going counter clockwise.
4. Post prompting questions in each section (see following image).

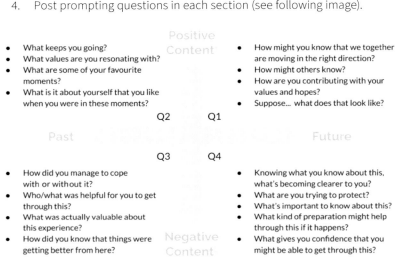

5. Invite team members to visit the quadrant where they want to start (first choice).
6. Once everyone has moved to a quadrant of their choice, invite people to turn to the person standing closest to them and have a conversation. They can take turns listening and asking the prompts (and adding their own if they are familiar and comfortable with coaching inquiries).
7. After approximately five minutes, invite everyone to move to their next quadrant of choice and repeat the process. Participants may choose to remain in the same quadrant.
8. (Optional) If time permits, facilitators may repeat the process until everyone has visited all four quadrants.
9. Invite the participants to go back to their seats and think of the following questions to share in a larger group wrap up:
   a. What became clearer for you as you had these conversations with your colleagues?
   b. What were some pleasant surprises for you?
   c. What ideas emerged from this experience that you would like to remember?
10. After a short reflecting break (1 minute), invite people to share.

Note: This is designed to be a standing exercise. Appropriate accommodation may be necessary based on the varying needs of each group.

Haesun Moon, PhD is a communication scientist and educator from the University of Toronto, Canada, and the author of *Coaching A–Z: The Extraordinary Use of Ordinary Words* (2022) and *Brief Coaching Handbook* (2019).

Note: Diagrams are reproduced with the agreement of Haesun Moon.

Systemic Coaching Questions

Ingredients

None

Description

'Systemic coaching' implies coaching with the system in mind. In other words, there is a shift in understanding who is the coaching client – from focusing solely on the individual towards *considering the client together with the system to which they belong* (e.g. their team or their organisation). The assumption behind this approach is that the challenges the person is facing are just consequences of a disturbance in the dynamics of the system. The client is just a 'symptom bearer' or 'systemic messenger' about the needs that are not met within the system. Consequently, when the flow and coherence in the client's system are restored, the individuals are freer to perform, connect with others, feel safer and maintain their sense of belonging in the system. This is well presented in Plato's words: "The part cannot be well unless the whole is well".

Like any other coach, systemic coaches use their stance, listening and asking questions. However, what is specific to this approach is that *the coach's listening goes beyond the individual and attends also to the system dynamics*. What is requested from the coach is to demonstrate two empathies: empathy for the individual and empathy for the system. While listening to the client that way, the coach might be wondering: "What is the story the system wants to tell here?", "What wants to be revealed?" or "What is blocking the free flow of the energy in this system?"

For a deeper understanding of this approach in coaching, it might be good to get familiar with the organising forces (also called systemic orders) that are necessary for a healthy and well-performing organisational system. The awareness of the systemic orders will provide you with useful guidance on where to listen and how to understand what the system needs to move forward.

When does it work best?

Systemic coaching and systemic questions work best when there is a feeling that what the client is experiencing is beyond their individual story. This approach might be particularly useful when working on blocking patterns or a sense of stuckness.

Step by step

This is not a recipe or a structured tool. True systemic questions occur in the moment, based on the established resonance with the person and their system. Nevertheless, to give you a flavour of how they might sound, here follows a list with some examples.

Systemic awareness of the client:
- With how many people do you feel connected when you say this? 5, 10, 100 or more?
- Who would be pleased to see you stuck like this?
- To whom do you remain loyal when you behave like this?
- For whom are you working so hard?

Exploring the blocking patterns in the organisation:
- How old is this pattern? Since when has this pattern existed?

Systemic Coaching Questions

- For what was this problem (pattern) once a solution?
- What does this pattern want to reveal or tell?
- What would not exist if the problem were not present?

Addressing the potential within the system:
- What wants to happen here?
- What is the greater learning that you are all learning in this situation?
- Where is life pulling you towards?
- What is the movement that wants to be completed?

Cooperation and belonging in the team:
- What are the unwritten rules of belonging in your company/team?
- What does it cost to belong to this team?
- What do you as a team need to sacrifice to be able to work together?
- What/who has not been seen or acknowledged enough in the past?

References

Bakker, S. (2019) *Moving Questions – How to Let Questions Work for You*.

Whittington, J. (2020) *Systemic Coaching and Constellations* (3rd edition). Kogan Page.

Darko Markovic is a systemic coach supporting organisations and leaders in making systemic changes and overcoming blocking patterns.

Supercharge Your Network

Ingredients

Pen and paper

Diagram (optional)

When does it work best?

This tool can be relevant at any career level, but is mostly applicable to clients in an early-to-mid-career stage or clients who have recently changed career or industry and find themselves in a new working environment. It can also be helpful in cases where clients feel uncomfortable or incapable of networking or navigating through company politics, and as a result express feelings of anger or annoyance, feeling overlooked for promotion or development opportunities.

Description

Careers happen in a social context. Connections and relationships are critical for everyone's success. We work alongside other people, learn from them, grow through interactions and challenges that work relationships offer, are influenced and influence our colleagues, build our skills and characters by working in teams, seek support and advice, learn about ourselves based on the feedback we receive and more. This tool focuses on the opportunity to leverage others' and our professional networks for learning and career growth. It provides the client with a greater level of awareness on how critical their network is and how they can utilise existing relationships and create new ones, and expand and build their network in a systematic manner, to help them grow professionally and progress their career.

Step by step

1. Ask the client to describe their career goal.
2. With this goal in mind, ask a series of questions, prompting the client to identify possible people to play one or more roles in their network:
   - Who will help you understand the organisation/industry and its culture? (Guide)
   - Who will help you increase your visibility within the organisation/ industry? (Promoter)

- Who will give you honest feedback on your performance? (Mirror)
- Who will continuously challenge you to develop further? (Challenger)
- Who will give you emotional support? (Confidante)
- Who will speak highly of you and your work? Who will sing your praises? (Cheerleader)
- Who has power to make things happen and move your ideas forward? (Sponsor)
- Who will help you learn from them and stretch your skills and knowledge? (Teacher)
- Who will help you connect to others? (Connector)
- Who can be/is a positive role model for your career? (Role model)
- Who will mentor you through personal and career decisions? (Mentor)

3. Ask the client to suggest any other role they think they need in their network and identify the person(s) to fill that role.
4. Ask the client to reflect on the gaps in the roles and identify actions to fill these gaps.
5. Work with the client to develop the plan for how to bring these people on board, to help them grow and progress.

Reference

Jones, G., and Gorell, R. (2018) *50 Top Tools for Coaching: A Complete Toolkit for Developing and Empowering People* (4ᵗʰ edition). London: Kogan Page.

Note: Diagrams are reproduced with the agreement of Jelena Jovanovic Moon.

Jelena Jovanovic Moon is a coach and psychologist, with degrees in coaching and organisational change and senior leadership roles in people management and organisational development.

Strengths-based Life Stories

Ingredients

Pen and paper

Description

Strength estrangement is a lack of awareness of one's strengths, or a lack of using one's strengths (Jones-Smith, 2013). Strengths-based life stories can help clients locate the source of their strengths and utilise them more effectively to achieve their desired goals.

The coach invites the client either to describe or, even better, to write their life story in three parts: past, present and future. Clients can be creative, but it is important to emphasise that their focus should be on their strengths in each of the three sections. The coach then reviews with the client each part of their life story, and draws out aspects which illustrates how they have used specific strengths to achieve successes.

When does it work best?

This tool works well when a client is unaware of their strengths. The tool enables the clients to build confidence by talking about positive experiences and linking these to attributes or strengths. From here the client can then explore how to use these strengths in the future.

Step by step

1. The coach invites the client to describe their life or a specific past success – something they are proud they have achieved. The focus in this exploration needs to be on positive actions taken by the client which led to the successful outcome, as opposed to more general and external factors (such as "I am proud of my children" or "I chose the numbers and we won £1,000 on the lottery").
2. Next, the coach invites the client to focus on a present-moment success.
3. In the third scenario, the coach invites the client to consider a future event and what attributes will contribute to the client's success.
4. The coach can use the tool within a session or as a homework task, inviting a client to write three different stories/events and to discuss these later. The choice will depend on the client and the nature of the work being undertaken.
5. Finally, in discussing these three stories, the coach encourages the client to explore their personal strengths, and how moving forward the client can play to these strengths, in what I often describe as "when playing football, you don't ask Ronaldo to be the goalkeeper". In other words, when you know what you are good at (in Ronaldo's case, taking free kicks and scoring goals) you find opportunities that allow you to maximise the potential of these strengths.

Reference

Jones-Smith, E. (2013) *Strengths-Based Therapy: Connecting Theory, Practice and Skills*. London: Sage.

Jonathan Passmore is a chartered psychologist, accredited master coach, team coach, supervisor, author and professor at Henley Business School.

Standing Up to Move Beyond Stuckness

Ingredients

None

When does it work best?

This technique works best when thinkers are stuck or going around in circles. They may not be able to see any new possibilities. It is especially useful if they are in their usual seat at their usual desk, as this will keep them stuck in their usual thinking patterns. But it can be equally useful if you are face to face and they appear to be stuck. It can also be used simply to see the situation from a different angle, to get a different perspective, from above (looking down at the situation) or from afar (looking at the horizon or at nature through a window).

Description

Standing up enhances attention (Rosenbaum et al., 2017). Those who work at standing desks are 12% more engaged than their seated colleagues (Dornhecker et al., 2015). Standing allows for optimum oxygen to reach the brain – an important prerequisite for creative thinking. The body takes in 11.5% more oxygen when standing compared to sitting (Froboese, n.d.).

Sitting still, in my experience, can cause thinkers (and coaches) to get stuck. The lack of physiological movement can lead to a lack of forward movement in thinking. This is especially true if the thinker is in the same seat that they sit in for their normal work, as that's often where the 'stuckness' was created in the first place.

Standing can help a thinker to see things from a new perspective, perhaps taking a helicopter view of the situation or a more visionary view if they are able to look out of the window.

Step by step

1. The coach invites the thinker into an experiment, explaining that standing up may give them a different perspective and asking them whether they would be willing to try it out.
2. Coach and thinker both stand (for equality's sake).
3. The coach asks: "What do you notice from this position that you didn't notice from your seat?" The word 'notice' is important here, so that they can access their preferred senses.
4. This never fails to lead to new thinking.
5. The coach may also ask the thinker to look out of a window, if one is close by: "What do you notice out on the horizon that you didn't notice before?" or "What do you notice out of the window that has a bearing on what you are thinking about here today?"
6. Again, this will lead to new insights.

References

Dornhecker, M., Blake, J.J., Benden, M., Zhao, H., and Wendel, M. (2015) The Effect of Stand-biased Desks on Academic Engagement: An Exploratory Study. *International Journal of Health Promotion and Education*, 53(5): 271–280.

Froboese, I. (n.d.) Zentrum für Gesundheit at Sports University Cologne.

Rosenbaum, D., Mama, Y., and Algom, D. (2017) Stand by Your Stroop: Standing Up Enhances Selective Attention and Cognitive Control. *Psychological Science*, 28(12): 1,864–1,867.

Clare Norman is an MCC ICF coach and a coaching supervisor.

SILENCE Model

Ingredients

None

When does it work best?

The SILENCE model can be widely applied, as the behaviours it outlines are an essential part of any effective coaching conversation and represent core coaching competencies. Holding the silence in this way can be especially impactful when the coach notices that the client is at a pivotal moment in the coaching and is experiencing a moment of deep reflection or personal inspiration.

Description

The ability to create and hold silence in a coaching conversation can be one of the hardest skills for a coach to master, and yet it has the power to totally transform coaching outcomes. This SILENCE model outlines seven steps the coach can take to create space and time for the magic of coaching to truly happen.

Step by step

1. *Slow down:* Don't rush. Ask a question, pause and wait for the client to respond, resisting the temptation to fill the silence. Slow the pace and give the client the opportunity to think without time pressure.
2. *Introspection:* Hold up a metaphorical mirror to create opportunities for reflective thought, and help the client look within to find their own answers.
3. *Listen:* True listening goes way beyond just hearing what the client is saying. Give full attention and don't interrupt or worry about the next question: by focusing on listening, the questions will naturally flow.
4. *Empathy:* Imagine what it is like to walk in the client's shoes, in order to fully understand their perspective. Build trust and openness by demonstrating empathy with their situation.
5. *Notice:* Be observant. Pay attention to the client's non-verbal cues, tone of voice and body language, and consider what they may be saying.
6. *Calm:* Use words, pace, tone and body language to create a calm, supportive and non-judgemental environment.
7. *Engage:* Switch off notifications and minimise external distractions to fully engage with the client and be totally present throughout the coaching.

By following these seven simple steps, the coach will be able to create a silence which is supportive, powerful and productive, giving the client the space and time to find their own path.

Rosie Nice is an executive coach, consultant and coaching trainer and author of *The Magic Happens in the Silence: A Guide to the Art of Reflective Coaching.*

Shared Values Tool to Map Values a Couple Share

Ingredients

A4 paper

Pencils/pens

When does it work best?

There is no optimal time to explore relationship values as there is always the potential for insight; however, this is not a good tool to use if the people involved are highly charged and unstable emotionally with each other.

It is important to note that it may be surprising, or even shocking, for clients to see that they don't neces-sarily share the same values as much as they had believed. This can generate some turbulent emotions, such as anger and grief.

Description

This technique has two main objectives. First, to assist your client in developing understanding of another person's values in relation to their own so that they can more consciously manage and develop that relationship. Second, to deepen a key relationship so that your client can access greater connection to meaning in their lives generally, arising from the relationship specifically.

Connection to meaning is a core driver of change, wellbeing and living a fulfilling life. The more we share meaning with others, the more we can draw on its beneficial energy. Being on the same page with a person you are in a relationship with is crucial for that relationship to thrive. It is also key in supporting change processes, if a person is in one (which we usually are!), and maintaining wellness generally. You don't have to be completely in alignment around values but there need to be enough *core* values shared so that you have sufficient common ground.

Oddly, many people in relationships have an unclear understanding or knowledge of the core values of those around them. People make assumptions about values and how they are ordered. This process is best used with both people in the room, usually because you are coaching them as a couple or one has been specifically invited to attend for the purposes of the exploration. If the couple are new clients, do not enter into this process until you have established a firm set of coaching agreements with them and after several coaching conversations.

Step by step

With both people in the coaching conversation present, proceed as follows.

1. Ask for and get agreement that 'no one gets to be wrong' and state that they may be surprised by what they discover about each other, as a way of preparing the ground.
2. Give them both a piece of paper and ask them to write down a list of what they currently consider to be their own values. If asked how many, guide them to between five and ten, but more is fine too. Give them ten minutes to do this.
3. On completion, ask them to review the list and reorder the items, putting their most important values at the top. These are core values. A quick way to guide them is to explain that core values are usually those that the person would find life unbearable to live without connection to and by. If that value were removed from their ability to live by it, they would experience considerable distress and even breakdown. They will end up

Shared Values Tool to Map Values a Couple Share

with a list that has their core values in order of importance from top to bottom of the page.

4. On completion, ask each in turn to read out their list, which both you and the other person agree simply to listen to without comment. Beforehand, prepare an A4 piece of paper orientated in landscape and divided into three equal parts vertically, making three columns.

5. As they read out their values, you, the coach, write down those values on this piece of A4 paper, one list to the left of the page for one person and the other to the right. As the values are read out you may hear values that are on both lists which can be written once in the centre column of your paper. Also, the non-core values that are shared are listed below the core values.

6. The central list represents where their values coincide. Those that are not on the list indicate where they differ.

7. As each person will have heard all the values read out loud, everyone will have knowledge of how many values are shared.

8. Coach the conversation to allow them to express their responses and emotions about the information.

9. Ask for agreement that they will not make any hasty or large decisions about their relationship until the process of integrating the information and learning has been completed through ongoing coaching with you or, should it become necessary, with other practitioners.

10. Design agreed assignments with them in relation to the process and pick those assignments up at the next conversation between you.

Anthony Eldridge-Rogers is a coach, facilitator, author and speaker specialising in Recovery and Wellness Coaching and the Meaning Centred Coaching model he created.

Diversity Circles (for Team Coaching)

Ingredients

Pens

Post It notes

A hat or similar receptacle

When does it work best?

The tool works best when team members may not previously have explored the various parts of their own personal identities together. A coach may note that, in pursuit of the team business goals, they have not really established psychological safety within the team and between members or explored how their diversity, both visible and invisible, can benefit the team's objectives.

Jonathan Drew MBE FRCP Edin is a leadership, career and team coach and a former British ambassador and ICF UK Chapter vice president.

Description

This model is used in team coaching to give team members different perspectives on diversity issues and improve team ways of working together and team purpose. It achieves this through increasing understanding between team members and working through what different individual team characteristics can mean for the team purpose, identity, values and beyond.

Step by step

1. Ask team members to think about one or more specific characteristics about themselves that they are okay to speak about (e.g. dyslexia, a particular religion or belief that they hold, their race, introversion, their gender).
2. Ask team members to write each of their suggestions on separate Post-it notes and place these in a hat.
3. Draw one out of the hat.
4. Ask the team to place themselves in two circles – one with the specific characteristic and one without the characteristic.
5. Those who are in the circle with the characteristic each have a chance to explain what the characteristic means to them within the context of work.
6. Those who are in the circle without the characteristic are asked to listen fully, without letting their own thoughts bubble up. After they have listened, they can ask questions in a sensitive manner.
7. The coach then asks for the two circles to join into one and asks two questions:
a) How can the team work better together as a result of what they have just heard and discussed?
b) How might they use the discussion and the better understanding of the diversity they now have to further improve their team purpose, identity or values – or beyond.
8. This can be repeated for each diversity characteristic – and the team can do this on their own once the first one has been facilitated by the coach.

ACCEPTS

Ingredients

Paper

Pens

Description

Dialectic behavioural therapy (DBT) is a therapeutic approach initially developed for clients with strong emotional urges, for example anger or sadness, which can be destructive. While there is little evidence of DBT being widely applied in coaching, many of the tools used in DBT can be useful when working with some types of coaching clients and some types of presenting issues.

ACCEPTS is a framework that can be easily applied in coaching conversations and used to support individual clients looking to create personal strategies to help themselves by distracting them from heightened emotions. ACCEPTS aims to help clients by distracting them from focusing on a trigger event and its associated emotions, by instead encouraging the client to focus on more positive situations. By focusing on more positive situations, clients may elicit feelings of joy and happiness, and in so doing, strengthen the pathways in their brain associated with the experience of pleasure, and reduce their experience both in the short and longer term of the negative emotions which cause them distress.

The acronym **ACCEPTS** stands for the following:
- **A**ctivities – engage in activities you enjoy
- **C**ontribution – to others and the community
- **C**omparisons – to others less fortunate or to worse situations you have been in
- **E**motions – engage in positive feelings and humour
- **P**ush away – put the situation to the side for a while
- **T**houghts – think about something else
- **S**ensations – experience a different intense feeling (e.g. take a cold shower, eat a spicy food)

When does it work best?

Dialectic behavioural therapy (DBT) works best to support clients who are struggling to manage strong emotional urges. These emotions in an organisational context are most likely to be anger, resulting from expectations not being meet, particularly in the performance of others, and where the individual holds a position of power where they are not directly accountable for their behaviour, such as a founder, owner or senior leader. The second emotion which some find overpowering is sadness. Sadness can result from job loss, loss of a close friend or partner, or business collapse. For some, this sadness can become overwhelming, meaning they can focus on little else. This technique can help the client, when used alongside other DBT approaches, to develop strategies to manage such overwhelming emotions.

Step by step

1. The coach describes the ACCEPTS model or offers a sheet of paper containing a table with the seven steps as headings over blank columns.
2. The coach invites the client to describe and capture in the table items or activities that might match one of the seven elements of ACCEPTS (see 'Description' above), until they have provided an item for each element.
3. As the client identifies each one, the coach encourages them to describe the situation in detail, with the aim of generating an emotional response associated with the memory.
4. The coach invites the client to test out in the coming week each of the seven aspects, and capture their thoughts about each on the table.
5. In the following session, the coach again explores the seven items and encourages the client to create a route where these seven experiences become a regular feature of their typical weekly routine.
6. A second review after a further month can both help to keep clients on track and also help them to recognise that some strategies are more helpful for some people than others; they should thus focus on the four or five that are most useful to them and that fit their routine and available time.

Jonathan Passmore is a chartered psychologist, accredited master coach, team coach, supervisor, author and professor at Henley Business School.

The Life Plan Review

Ingredients

None

When does it work best?

The Life Plan Review works best when people have set goals, but want to find a way to track their effort. By focusing on effort ("my best"), the process recognises the difference between what's inside our control and what's not. I can run "my best" race, break the world record (these are inside my control), but someone else might run faster than me (this is outside my control). It's for this reason that elite athletes focus on running their best race, not winning, as we cannot control others. In life we can be satisfied, if we have done our best.

Description

The Life Plan Review (Goldsmith, 2022) aims to help clients close the gap between what they plan to do with their life and what actually gets done. It presumes that they have decided already what they want their goal or life plan to be. But unlike other goal-management techniques, this technique is aimed at goal delivery, as opposed to goal setting. It invites the coach (or the client can do it themselves) to set up a regular time in their schedule and conduct a weekly self-audit. It's also different, as while most goal tools focus on what has been achieved, this one focuses on what's inside the individual's control (effort). It invites the client to review six questions each day.

Have I done my best today to:
1. … set clear goals?
2. … make progress towards each goal?
3. … find meaning?
4. … be happy?
5. … maintain and build positive relationships?
6. … be fully engaged?

Step by step

1. **Set clear goals** The starting point for a performance-management process is to set one's goals. The best goals are those that have personal meaning for us, contribute to our happiness, are in line with our values, are future focused, within our control (or at least within our immediate influence), are measurable and combine a long-term aim with intermediate steps. The coach should aim to check the client has established goals that meet these criteria.
2. **Track each day** The coach should invite the client to establish a time each day, maybe 10 minutes at the close of the day, to review their performance. They should do this by noting their answers to each of the six questions.
3. **Arrange a weekly meeting or review** The coach can invite the client to create a regular time in their diary to review their goals. This can be self-monitoring or a weekly meeting with their coach. In fact, based on experience, most people enjoy connection and know they are more likely to complete the review if someone joins them in the process.
4. **Review the goals and effort each week** In reviewing progress, the insights provide useful data for review. Maybe the client is not setting clear goals or these goals are not creating happiness, meaning or outcomes. If that's the case, what needs to change? Such insights lead back to reflection and a further coaching conversation.

Reference

Goldsmith, M. (2022) *The Earned Life*. London: Penguin Press.

Marshall Goldsmith is recognised as the world-leading executive coach and is the *New York Times* best-selling author of many books including *The Earned Life*, *Triggers*, *Mojo* and *What Got You Here Won't Get You There*.

Career Lessons

Ingredients

Pen and paper

When does it work best?

The exercise revisits the past to offer lessons for the future. Therefore, it works best when a client expresses a sense of dissatisfaction about their career progress to date, or regret that they are not further up the career ladder, feeling that their aspirations are slipping, goals becoming less attainable or out of their control. This tool is especially helpful when a client lacks under-standing on how they ended up where they are, compared to their career ambitions.

Description

This tool helps clients to get a broader perspective on their career to date, with the purpose of learning from past experiences. The goal is to offer the client an opportunity to gain awareness of career lessons from their past, so they have clarity on the decision-making that brought them here. This should give them a sense of control over their career and empower future decisions. Gained awareness of common themes from the past builds momentum for them to take ownership over their career, proactively creating opportunities and driving progression.

The coach guides the client through their career journey step by step, revisiting each of their career decisions until they reach the present time. The tool invites the client to reflect on career choices they have made, the career direction they took and factors they considered relevant in making career decisions. The client looks back on their education and their choices over consecutive roles they took as stepping stones, all the way to their current position. The exercise results in a chronological map of the client's career, giving them a greater perspective and enabling them to identify the common themes in their career choices.

Step by step

Phase 1: Revisiting the past

1. Ask the client to write down choices made early in their career. Refer to their choice of education: what did they choose and why? What were the other options they considered? Did they have any help or advice in making the decision? Then ask them how they reflect on those decisions from today's perspective: what do they feel and think about the choices made? Would they make the same or different choices now? What do they wish they had known at the time?

2. Ask the client about their first role. Ask them to reflect on the decision-making at the time: what led them to make that decision? What other options did they have? Did they get any advice? How do they feel about it now? Would they have made the same choice? Do they think this choice opened up or restricted their future career choices?

3. Follow the same set of questions from role to role, until you reach the present time. Let the client decide if they would prefer to go through every single role or only the key roles that defined their career journey to date.

Career Lessons

Phase 2: Identifying key themes from the past

4. Ask the client to take a step back and reflect on their career journey and decisions: what are the key themes that emerge about the type of choices they made, the decision-making process, the factors that influenced the decisions, proactivity vs. reactivity in career progress, their clarity of goals and plans to achieve them? Ask them what they wish they had done differently, what are the common factors in the decisions they feel good about and what for those they regret, and what are the features of the environments in which they were more or less successful?

Phase 3: Applying lessons from the past to the future

5. Ask the client to consider a long-term career goal: their north star.
6. Ask the client to think about their short-term career future and what decisions they will likely have to make in the next one-to-two years: how much clarity do they have over their career goals? How can they specify these? How do these sit against known and possible business change scenarios? How can one or more of these scenarios be used for career development, as a stepping stone towards their career goals? Ask the client to think how short-term career decisions could expand or limit their future career choices.
7. Ask the client what lessons learnt they can use to prepare better for future decision-making: how well do they know themselves? What are the values that drive them and their decision-making? How can they apply these in career decisions? How can they utilise their support network? Where could they seek advice and get information?
8. Ask the client how you can help them along the journey. It is possible the client will want to think and reflect on this further, and that follow-up sessions would be beneficial to create an action plan.

Reference

Lancer, N., Clutterback, D., and Megginson, D. (2016) *Techniques for Coaching and Mentoring* (2nd edition). Abingdon: Routledge.

Jelena Jovanovic Moon is a coach and psychologist, with degrees in coaching and organisational change and senior leadership roles in people management and organisational development.

What's the Evidence?

Ingredients

Reflective journal/ notepad

When does it work best?

What's the Evidence? is particularly useful for a client who has repeated behavioural patterns that they wish to change, but which are deeply held – for example, an individual who likes to please others and finds it hard to say no, but finds themselves feeling overwhelmed and unfocused. It also works with clients who ruminate on something that happens at work, playing out alter-native scenarios, and are unable to let it go. Some situations loom large but actually occur infrequently, and by gathering evidence, it can be reframed as less of a problem.

Description

What's the Evidence? is a tool to be used between coaching sessions to help a client to gather evidence about the issue they are struggling with, and to aid them in unpicking the details and developing alternative perspectives. The client is asked to keep a written journal over a period of time and, when the situation arises, to document the thoughts, feelings, actions and outcomes associated with an issue. The client captures data on which to reflect further, to understand the impact of the issue, and to think through alternative narratives or ways to respond. Returning to the journal after recording the evidence for a period of time allows the client to reframe the issue within its wider context and to understand its magnitude. The evidence that the client documents around the topic can also be discussed during a coaching conversation.

Step by step

1. Ask if the client is interested in capturing data about the issue under discussion.
2. Explain that the process of journalling, as the situation arises, will provide timely information about the issue that can be used to help to clarify thinking and allow for other perspectives or an alternative way of doing things to arise.
3. Ask them to write down details of the issue as soon as possible after it has occurred. What was the trigger? What were the thoughts, emotions and bodily sensations associated with the situation? How did they respond? What was the outcome?
4. The act of writing as the situation occurs facilitates a clearer record and can help with letting go of some of the negative thinking and feelings that accompany the situation.
5. For example, a client who finds it hard to say no is asked to take on a new project when they are already at capacity. They feel a sense of being overwhelmed as well as anger that their manager is not aware of their current workload, and resentment towards a colleague who seems to have more time and is rarely asked to take on extra projects. The client writes down these thoughts and emotions, the situation that led to them and how they responded.
6. Suggest that they review the journal entry a few days later and write down what new ideas occur to them now, with the perspective of time. What are they now thinking and feeling? How can these insights be used to experiment with a new way of reacting or behaving? Perhaps they can write an alternative scenario that results in a preferred outcome.
7. For example, with a client who finds it hard to say no, a new emotion of disappointment in themselves came up and a realisation that they

hadn't talked through their priorities with their manager. They recognised that they could have said no or asked more questions. They wrote
down a new intention for how they will respond in the future to a similar
situation.

8. Ask the client to keep a journal for a week, a month or longer, depending
on the issue, and the frequency with which it arises.

9. During a future coaching conversation, ask the client how they have
found the process of journalling their issue and what new ideas, insights
and intentions have arisen as a result (see the Four 'I's tool on page XX).

Sarah Gledhill is an
accredited coach who
specialises in the higher
education and non-profit
sectors, following an
international fundraising
career.

Anchoring Positive Feelings

Ingredients

None

When does it work best?

The technique works best in coaching when a client is responding negatively, or perhaps not as positively as they would like, in particular situations. For this, they set an anchor that triggers a positive response internally and behaviourally. When the situation arises in future, they can activate their anchor and respond in their new, chosen manner. Equally, the anchor can be activated at any time where the chosen response is wanted. This could be simply to change from feeling unhappy to feeling very happy.

Description

The anchor method is a stimulus-response technique. The 'anchor' is something that triggers a response in us. That response can be internal or external, physical or behavioural – for example, feeling annoyed when someone you dislike comes into the room, or picking up the phone when it rings. Think about how you can suddenly feel so good when something triggers the memory of a loved one or a wonderful situation. Generally speaking, these anchors lie in our subconscious minds and we are allowing ourselves to be controlled by them. We can use this neuroscience-informed approach to change how we feel through the use of a stimulus. If a trigger sets this off based on a memory from the past, we can create our own trigger for a chosen response.

Step by step

1. The coach asks the client to choose how they would want to feel or behave in a particular situation. (For example, feeling positive and happy as you walk into an office to meet a customer or feeling confident in a board meeting.)
2. The coach asks the client to relax and remember a time when they had that feeling before. It doesn't have to relate to a future selected situation, simply an experience of the feeling itself. Anchoring works best when you pick a strong feeling.
3. The coach asks the client to close their eyes and remember how good/powerful this felt at the time. Let them enjoy the moment here for a minute or two. Tell them that they can increase the intensity of this experience by:
   a. Picturing the situation in their mind
   b. Hearing any voices associated with it
   c. Hearing music associated with it
   d. Making the colours brighter
   e. Making the sounds clearer
   f. Thinking of a word that enhances the feeling (for example, 'wow', 'great', etc.).
4. This is when they create their anchor, while the feeling is most intense.
5. Tell them that their anchor is simply a physical movement or gesture (for example, squeezing their thumb, touching their shoulder, squeezing their middle finger and thumb together or touching their earlobe). It works best if this is a simple move that others won't be likely to notice.
6. Let them know that as the feeling fades, they can release their anchor and relax and take a few deep breaths.
7. After a few moments, ask them to repeat the process a few times to increase the strength of their anchor.

Anchoring
Positive Feelings

8. For increased strength, ask them if they can choose a different memory of having had that same feeling, then they can repeat the procedure (steps 3–5).
9. It's really important that you use the same gesture/touch every time.
10. If they can, then ask them to choose a third example and anchor the feeling to the same gesture.
11. Suggest they trigger their anchor by the touch/gesture several times over the coming hours and days, and check if the feeling comes back. It should soon become automatic.
12. If the feeling is not intense enough, repeat the procedure.
13. Once their anchor has been deeply set, it will last a lifetime. It will be there whenever they want to change their feelings or behaviour.

Phil Summerfield is a master practitioner coach-mentor with a focus on executive and team coaching. He is a member of the Marshall Goldsmith 100 Coaches organisation.

Moving from Resilience to Antifragility

Ingredients

Paper

Pencils/pens

When does it work best?

This approach works well when a client is talking about a difficult, challenging situation in their lives and they are tilting towards trying to resist the situation and apply resistance to it. Almost everyone can grasp this idea once it is set out to them. This process can sometimes inspire people to make hasty decisions. If pursuing antifragility rather than resilience becomes an apparent choice, take your time to explore it over a few sessions.

Description

This powerful technique seeks to assist a client to shift from a defensive position, where they seek to stop personal change occurring as a result of life forces and experiences, and return to a previous condition or status quo. Instead, we want to encourage them to explore actively seeking the benefits of healthy stress and so decide to accept and endure short-term stresses or suffering for larger beneficial goals. This profitable growth from stress is called antifragility, as opposed to resilience.

Resilience is the capacity of a person to bounce back to an original condition or way of being. A highly resilient person can suffer pressures and stresses at significant levels but can quickly recover to their former condition. They are good at resisting these forces and are not changed by them. This is a 'good' in some, but not all, contexts.

Antifragility is different. In people it means that they are changed and made stronger by life's shocks and stressors. They revert, not to a former condition, but to a new, changed, more useful, stronger condition. Resilience then is not something that we want to apply to all of life. To do that would be to stifle life completely. We are interactive beings who can gain considerably from stress and forces that act on us and make us uncomfortable or cause us to suffer.

The coaching process is about change. No one enters coaching to stay the same. Performance is about change too but there can be no increase in performance without both change and, if it is to be sustained, antifragility. A simple example of antifragility is how we improve muscle strength. Exercising muscles to cause them to strengthen and grow involves causing them low levels of harm, breaking and tearing the tissue. The body naturally responds to this deliberate 'harm' by rebuilding the muscle and adding additional muscle mass. It does this as a response to the 'harm' to provide for an improved response the next time the muscle experiences the stress of being torn or damaged.

Step by step

1. When your client presents a topic where they are feeling like they have to be resilient and apply resistance, suggest this process.
2. Invite your client to list all of the ways that they can resist the situation or experience. Tell them you will make a list for the purpose of exploration later in the session. Once they have produced a list, which is best kept to five items or so, read it back to them slowly. Enquire as to how each of the items makes them feel when they hear the feedback. For each item, ask them to evaluate how much of their personal energy, focus, attention and resources it will use up.

_Moving from
Resilience to
Antifragility_

3.   Once this conversation feels complete, ask them to consider what will happen if they make a choice not to resist or apply resilience to the situation. What if they decide not to fight it? To let it change them.

4.   Then go through the list again and this time ask them to make another list of what the opposite of each item is.

5.   Using a 'what will happen then and what might you learn?' approach in coaching questioning for each item on the list, explore this alternative response. Listen carefully for where there may be opportunities for them to develop experience and to learn. Use coaching skills of challenge to call them into a place of imagined new strength that they might find in themselves.

6.   Although this alternative response may involve perceived or actual suffering and risk, explore the benefits that could be gained from the experience. Consider what the new choice can open up in them, as a person and in their life options, together with how the new path might strengthen them in new ways.

Reference

Taleb, N.N. (2012) _Antifragile Things that Gain from Disorder._ New York, NY: Reactions Publishing Group Ltd.

Anthony Eldridge-Rogers is a coach, facilitator, author and speaker specialising in Recovery and Wellness Coaching and the Meaning Centred Coaching model he created.

Writing a Review of the Future

Ingredients

None

Description

This is a simple technique that involves writing a 'review' of a future imagined activity or achievement, such as that best-selling novel or business book, or memorable conference speech. It helps clients understand more about themselves and their imagined goal, helping them to take a different perspective on their future achievements and success.

Step by step

1. Once a client has identified something that they may like to work towards, ask them to imagine that it has come to fruition, for example: "imagine that your novel has recently been published and the reviews are starting to flood in".
2. Either in the session or as potential pre-work or homework, ask the client to write a review of the accomplishment. The client can interpret this however they wish. Perhaps the review suggests that it has been a great success or perhaps it is more critical. It could take the form of a review in the Sunday papers (such as for a book) or a client testimonial (such as for a course).
3. Work with the client through an open coaching conversation to see what stood out for them and what they have learned, and what this means for their next steps.

When does it work best?

This interactive and thought-provoking exercise is helpful for clients who may be undecided about whether to commit time to a specific time-consuming project or goal (such as publishing a book or developing a new training course). They may also be stuck and finding it difficult to get motivated to develop their ideas. By asking them to write a review of their achievement, as if they were an objective outsider, the client can work through what they would like to get out of the project, and find most meaningful about it. They may also be helped to decide whether it is worth pursuing by being invited, in an experiential way, to envision what the future they are striving for might feel like.

Julie Flower is a leadership development coach, consultant and facilitator, with a specialism in improvisation in complex systems. She is also an external tutor in executive coaching at Henley Business School.

Unpicking with Picture Metaphors

Ingredients

A3 paper

Coloured pens

A whiteboard (optional)

When does it work best?

It's useful to use this technique at any stage in a coaching conversation but especially so in the reality phase to understand and increase awareness about the situation and the client's perception of it.

References

Merriam-Webster (2017) Metaphor. Available from: https://www.merriam-webster.com/dictionary/metaphor

Passmore, J. (2022) The Role of Metaphor in Coaching. *The Coaching Psychologist*, 18(2): 44–46. Available from: https://doi.org/10.53841/bpstcp.2022.18.1.44.

Westbrook, D., Kennerley, H., and Kirk, J. (2017) *An Introduction to Cognitive Behaviour Therapy* (3rd edition). London: Sage.

Description

Often clients will use an interesting metaphor, simile or analogy when trying to describe an obstacle, goal, issue or circumstance (Passmore, 2022). A metaphor is defined as "a figure of speech in which a word or phrase literally denoting one kind of object or idea is used in place of another, to suggest a likeness or analogy between them" (Merriam-Webster, 2017). An example could be "it's been a complete circus at work since our boss announced he's retiring". Sometimes, replaying these to a client can help to create further thoughts.

Metaphors and analogies temporarily change the focus from the topic at hand to a parallel situation, shifting the emotion and enabling more productive thinking (Westbrook, Kennerley and Kirk, 2017). This exercise goes beyond by requesting the client to illustrate the metaphor they employed, in order to create a richer conversation and comprehension. The metaphor provides a concise way of communicating otherwise-complex information. Drawing the metaphor then pulls out further details of what is under the surface of the use of the metaphor.

Step by step

1. Replay the metaphor used by the client back to them. Ask the client if they want to explore this further. If yes, ask the client to draw what they just described when they used this metaphor. If working remotely, this can be done using a whiteboard, and rather than drawing, different images can be pasted here.
2. Encourage the client to include as much detail as possible. Allow plenty of time for this.
3. Discuss what it represents and the various options and possibilities related to this. Stay with the metaphor as much as possible. For example, if thinking of the problem as bees on a tree, the initial line of questions should be within this scenario: what would happen to the bees if someone chopped the tree down? What could the bees do? What else could be happening in this same landscape?
4. After exploring the metaphor, relate it to the problem at hand. For example, who are the bees within your situation? Who is the tree in your situation? Which options seem best for you?
5. This can be used later in the session, or in subsequent sessions, to continue the exploration or measure progress.
6. Once the client is ready, continue the session as you normally would.

Claudia Day is a coach and entrepreneur, co-founder of My Coaching Place, part of the AC UK leadership team, and holds a master's in coaching and behavioural change (Henley) and a master's in business administration (MIT).

Cartooning in Coaching

Ingredients

Sheets of paper (at least A4 size and enough for several attempts, where necessary)

A variety of coloured pens and markers, including black (Bold black outlines make for stronger images – especially when working online.)

When coaching online: client's phone camera (for photographing their cartoon and displaying it via a shared screen)

Description

Some cartoons make you laugh out loud. Some cartoons don't – but they point up absurdities, causing a wry smile of recognition in the process. Cartoonists, particularly political cartoonists, draw on five key elements to create impact:

1. **Analogy** – a comparison between two unlike things that share some characteristics.
2. **Symbolism** – using an object to represent an idea.
3. **Irony** – the difference between the way things are and the way things should be or are expected to be.
4. **Exaggeration** – overstating or magnifying a problem, physical feature or habit.
5. **Labelling and captioning** – to clarify an idea.

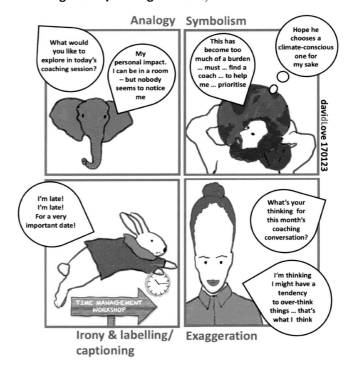

Scott McCloud, a maker of comics, highlights the importance of amplification through simplification: the stripping down of the visualisation of a subject to its essential elements can amplify meaning in a way that representational art cannot. We can use this idea through cartooning in coaching to enable clients to get down to the fundamentals of a situation they wish to explore. Cartooning is a powerful means of storytelling – it's not just a form of sketching, it's a way of *seeing* that can offer a new window onto a situation.

Cartooning in Coaching

When does it work best?

When the client is stuck and a radically different lens will be helpful. To explore more deeply a Freudian slip made by the client – or a metaphor they have introduced. When the client exhibits a sense of humour about the topic being explored – or life in general.

As the coach, you need to feel confident and have the capability to work productively with any strong emotions that can arise for the client when using art-based approaches.

Cartoons in coaching offer opportunities to:
- Create caricatures
- Illustrate the pantomime nature of some aspects of organisational life
- Invoke satire as a way of understanding challenging situations
- Exaggerate and subvert stereotypes
- Make connections to important systemic factors
- Unearth influential aspects of organisational culture – or life more generally.

Simple elements can combine in complex ways and, when supported by a coaching conversation, can be a powerful source of insight. More broadly, we know that humour has positive health and wellbeing impacts.

Step by step

1. Contract carefully about using a cartooning approach: pay attention to the client's possible reticence – they may have concerns about a 'childish' or 'comic-like' approach, they may need convincing of the benefits or they may believe they have no creative skill. Reassure them that anything goes and encourage a playful, *child-like* attitude. Bear in mind, it's always an invitation, which may involve encouragement to suspend disbelief.

2. Emphasise that we can all create cartoons using basic shapes (e.g. circles, ovals, squares, rectangles, triangles and diamonds). We can all doodle stick figures and use dots and lines to make simple but expressive faces. We can add speech and thought bubbles to add further observations and humour. Brief captions can help to explain or highlight what's going on in the image – but encourage the client to keep words to a minimum.

3. Confirm that the end result only needs to make sense to them and will be treated confidentially.

Further reading and references

Chapman, R. (2012) *Drawing Comics Lab.* Beverley, Massachussetts: Quarry Books.

Elliman, J. (2016) What Happens in Moments of Humour with My Clients? In E. de Haan (ed.), *Behind Closed Doors – Stories from the Coaching Room.* London: Libri Publishing.

Gash, J. (2017) *Coaching Creativity – Transforming your Practice.* Abingdon: Routledge.

Gregory, A. (2006) *The Creative License – Giving Yourself Permission to be the Artist You Truly Are.* New York: Hachette Books.

McCloud, S. (2006) *Understanding Comics* and *Making Comics.* New York: Harper.

Sheather, A. (2019) *Coaching Beyond Words – Using Art to Deepen and Enrich Our Conversations.* Abingdon: Routledge.

Watts, A. (2022) *Collage as a Creative Coaching Tool – A Comprehensive Resource for Coaches and Psychologists.* Abingdon: Routledge.

Note: Cartoons supplied by David Love and reproduced with his permission.

4. Ask the client if they have a favourite cartoonist. What do they like about that person's approach? What particular characteristics of their cartoons is the client drawn to?

5. Invite the client to think about what cartoonists do – particularly political cartoonists, because they focus on issues. They:
   - Juxtapose (sometimes contradictory) ideas
   - Find humour in everything – even the darkest topics
   - Point out the absurdities of a situation… or life in general
   - Notice patterns and discrepancies
   - Cut straight to the essence of a topic
   - Mine metaphors for their significance
   - Create caricatures and satire
   - Sketch in unrealistic or semi-realistic ways
   - Generate an immediate impact
   - Develop a strong narrative.

6. The following process steps are based on Anna Sheather's Five Stages of Coaching with Art (Sheather, 2019, pp.78–87).

7. Visualisation: encourage the client to focus on the topic they want to explore and allow a cartoon image to form in their heads (a meditative exercise can be very helpful here – or quiet contemplation accompanied by a piece of calming music).

8. Give the client a maximum of 10 minutes to create their cartoon. Encourage them to capture the first image that comes to mind, rather than spend time analysing what's emerging (analysis will come later in the conversation). Try to organise things so you can observe *how* they go about the creative process.

9. Ask the client to talk through the cartoon they have created. It is *their* interpretation of the cartoon that's important – not yours! Invite the client to consider the different elements of the cartoon and their sequencing in the overall narrative. Sheather's approach offers great ways to enable a client to explore an image in depth, focusing on, for example: the size and positioning of characters and objects; what you noticed about the process the client used; the energy with which they approached the task; the order things were added to the cartoon; and anything, with hindsight, they might perceive as missing.

10. Explore how the client has deployed humour, symbolism, exaggeration, irony, analogy, labelling, caricature and satire. What significance do these features have for the client's coaching goal? What are the wider impacts on relationships with others? What might be the systemic implications? Enable the client to identify the insights and learning gained from the activity and how these apply in their world. What will the client now do with these insights?

David Love is a leadership coach and supervisor/mentor and the 'house' cartoonist with the Association for Coaching magazine, *Coaching Perspectives*

*Collective
Thinking*

Step by step

1. Gather the team together and describe the process, rules and objectives of a timed-talk brainstorm session.
2. Appoint a scribe, who will collect the ideas on a board or flipchart. Set an overall time limit, depending on the complexity of the problem. As coach, you will be the timekeeper.
3. Begin with a challenge or topic discussion or brief.
4. Flip a coin to decide who goes first and then set a timer for three minutes. Ask the person selected to go first to start by simply talking for the three minutes about the topic. Encourage diagrams and Post-its to bring ideas to life and help others see things in different ways and encourage weird and wacky ideas.
5. Take turns talking, three minutes each.
6. Do not allow interruptions or the taking over of someone else's turn – no matter what.
7. Ask the participant to stop talking the instant the timer goes off.
8. Take as many turns as necessary to get as many ideas as possible. Sifting and sorting come later.
9. To close the activity, discuss with the group how ideas and opportunities can be best captured and taken forward from the discussion. This should ideally be at a separate event/time to ensure the focus is on the creating of ideas.

Reference

Kline, N. (1999) *Time to Think: Listening to Ignite the Human Mind*. London: Cassell.

Maggie Grieve is an accredited leadership and team development coach, consultant and facilitator with 30 years of working with organisa-tions and leaders across the world. She owns her own business, Ping Thinking, and is an external coach for NHS England.

OSKAR

Ingredients

None

References

Grant, A.M. (2012) Making Positive Change: A Randomized Study Comparing Solution-focused vs. Problem-focused Coaching Questions. *Journal of Systemic Therapies*, 31(2): 21–35.

McKergow, M., and Jackson, P.Z. (2002) *The Solutions Focus: Making Coaching and Change SIMPLE*. Boston, USA: Nicholas Brealey International.

Description

OSKAR (McKergow and Jackson, 2002) is a framework drawn from solution-focused therapy and is a great way to redirect conversations away from the problem and to encourage people to focus on the solution. OSKAR is a mnemonic and the letters stand for: Outcome, Scale, Know-how, Affirm and Review. Like other coaching approaches, the framework encourages the individual to focus their thinking on the aspects of the problem that are inside their control, and to consider their own knowledge, skills and personal strengths to help them move towards a solution. Research evidence from a randomised control trial that compared solution-focused with problem-focused coaching questions (Grant, 2012) suggests that the approach can be a highly effective way to support individuals to meet their goals as well as improve self-efficacy.

Step by step

1. Outcome or objective: The first step is to establish with the individual what they are trying to achieve. In doing so, it's always better to focus on moving towards a goal (approach goals) over moving away from a goal – for example, "I want a healthier diet" rather than "I want to give up eating chocolate".

2. Scale: Invite the person to rate how determined they are to achieve their goal on a 1–10 scale. As a rough guide, determination scores below 7 often mean that the individual will lack the motivation to move forward. As a result, the coach may wish to explore what would need to be addressed in order to increase their level of determination to change.

3. Know-how: The next step is to explore the existing knowledge the person already holds about the solutions available. Returning to the example, do they know what a 'healthy diet' is, what foods it contains, in what quantities and how frequently they should be eaten? The individual may need to do some further research to discover more insights, maybe by talking to others, reading or searching the internet.

4. Affirm and action: At this stage the aim is to identify one or more actionable steps that the individual wishes to take to move them closer towards their goal – the solution. Once again, at this stage of the process, scaling can be used to help the individual identify both their priorities and their confidence.

5. Review: The review stage can be used to reflect back on progress made, in the following discussion, and to ask questions such as "What have you done?" and "How has it helped move towards your goal?" The process can then be repeated to identify new actions.

Emily Barber is a coach and experienced project manager who coordinates the work of the CoachHub research lab.

ELI5

Ingredients

Optionally, some colour pens and paper

Description

'ELI5' stands for 'explain like I'm five' and is a slang term that originated on the Reddit platform. It is commonly used on the internet, particularly on social media and forums, to request an explanation of a complex topic or concept in a simple and easy-to-understand way. The idea behind ELI5 is to break down complex ideas into simple, easy-to-digest language and examples that a five-year-old child could understand. Simple drawings can also be used. This can help make difficult concepts more accessible to people who may not have a background in the subject matter. The real benefit is, however, for the client, as the technique is an invitation to think about their challenges in a simpler, easier-to-grasp way. It helps clients to focus on the essentials and bring more structure in content that could otherwise be overwhelming.

When does it work best?

Coaches can apply the ELI5 technique to help clients simplify their thoughts or language during a coaching session when the client is having difficulty articulating clearly or when the coach feels that the client is getting bogged down in too much detail. Simplifying can help the client to better understand their own thoughts and feelings and can make it easier for the coach to understand and address the client's concerns.

Additionally, the ELI5 technique can be useful when a client is struggling to identify the core issue or goal they want to work on. By breaking things down to the basics, they can often see what is most important.

Simplifying can also be helpful when a client is feeling overwhelmed or stressed, as it can help them to focus on the most important things and take action.

In summary, ELI5 is a technique that coaches might use to help clients to better understand and communicate their thoughts, feelings and goals, and to focus on the most important aspects of a situation.

Step by step

1. Check with your client whether simplifying the situation would be helpful for them and whether they would mind re-explaining their challenge in a different way. It's important that this is not about 'child's play' but rather about going back to the essence.
2. Ask your client to explain their challenge as if they were speaking to a five-year-old. Offer them drawing paper and colouring pens if they think it might be helpful.
3. Challenge your client as if you were the five-year-old on the complexity of structure and concepts they use in their descriptions. As a coach you really need to help them break down all complexity so that a five-year-old really could understand it.
4. Discuss the essential concepts and structure that came out of this with the client.

Marc Innegraeve is an accredited executive and team coach and a researcher. He holds an MSc in coaching and behavioural change from Henley.

Career Manifesto

Ingredients

Pen and paper

When does it work best?

This tool can be used at any point in a client's career. It is particularly helpful when people feel they are stuck in their career or are at a crossroads, or feel time is slipping and they are confused about where they want to head to. This is often the case when people let their career 'happen' to them, rather than being in the driving seat. The career manifesto offers them a step-by-step approach to clarify their aspirations and create a roadmap to achieve them.

Description

Achieving clarity on a long-term goal and where they are aiming helps people to realise their true potential. It brings focus, identification of next steps and motivation for action, and is a lens to be used when considering options; it also provides an understanding of relevant interdependencies, support to be secured and obstacles to be overcome. Research evidence suggests that having a documented career plan significantly increases the likelihood of career success.

The coach uses this tool to guide the client through the creation of their long-term career plan. The tool itself is very simple, the value being added through the structure it brings to the career-planning process. It gives the client a step-by-step approach to think about their career in an organised manner, resulting in clarity of goals and leading to an action plan. The exercise starts with a long-term vision for the client's career, or in other words their career 'north star'. Identification of their north star helps the client to focus on what matters to them in the long term and to identify opportunities for advancement toward it. It also helps any decision-making along the way so that short-term and mid-term decisions are made with the end goal in mind.

A career plan is not a one-off exercise and the plan is rarely set in stone. Flexibility must be embedded in it and it should be revisited regularly, because aspirations, interests, circumstances and plans change. The plan must work for the client, rather than forcing the client to follow the original plan blindly. The coach helps the client create a plan and then encourages them to review the plan on a regular basis.

Step by step

1. Ask the client how far ahead they want to plan (i.e. what is the period they have in mind – for example, three, five or 10 years?).
2. Ask them to project/imagine themselves into that period and be as specific as possible about the details:
   - What sort of company are they working for?
   - What role are they doing?
   - What seniority/level do they have?
   - Are they managing a team – and if so, how big?
   - What are they earning?
   - What is the atmosphere in the company and company culture?
   - What does their typical day at work look like?
   - How have they grown as a person and professionally – how would they describe themselves?

Career Manifesto

3. With the described goal role in mind, ask them to think of the skills and competencies they will need for that role.
4. Ask them to compare these with those they have at the moment.
   - Which of their current skills/competencies are transferable?
   - Which of the skills/competencies would they need to develop further?
   - Where are the gaps and how big are these on a scale of 1–10 for each of the required skills/competencies?
5. Ask them what else they need to explore, research or find out in order to finalise the plan.
6. Working backwards from the defined end goal, ask them to break down their career plan into milestones.
7. Work with the client on an action plan for achieving the first milestone.
8. Review the plan with them on a regular basis or encourage them to do it themselves.

Reference

Jones, G., and Gorell, R. (2018) *50 Top Tools for Coaching: A Complete Toolkit for Developing and Empowering People* (4th edition). London: Kogan Page.

Jelena Jovanovic Moon is a coach and psychologist, with degrees in coaching and organisational change and senior leadership roles in people management and organisational development.

Who is in Charge of Who? Conversations with a Mobile Phone

Ingredients

Client's mobile phone

A chair or chairs

Description

The mobile phone has caught our attention. Many people have had their attention hijacked by mobile devices to the extent that the phone now rules aspects of their attention and behaviour. This is an exercise for individuals about their relationship with their mobile device that will make it more explicit and can revise the locus of control to the benefit of the client. It is deliberately supposed to be light-hearted and fun but can yield some interesting and important insights about relationships.

Step by step

1. Get consent from your client to explore their relationship with technology, in particular their mobile device. Explain that this will be light-hearted and involve some role play.
2. Ask them to put their phone upright on a chair facing them, with the mobile turned on but on silent.
   Ask them, "If your phone was a person, would they be male, female or neither?" Ask them to give the phone a name. Thereafter, refer to the phone by this name. For the purpose of this example, let's say they have named the phone "Jane". You may get some resistance as this can feel silly to some, but usually it is playful and humorous, turning to thoughtful.
3. Proceed to ask the following kinds of questions, using your own wording and order:
   "How do you feel about Jane?"
   "In what ways does Jane assist you in your life?"
   "What value does Jane add?"
   "Does Jane ever become a nuisance?"
   "How much control do you feel you have over Jane?"
   "If you could change Jane, in what ways would you do that?"
   "How does Jane get in the way of things in your life, if at all?"
   "How easy is it for you not to be with Jane?"
   As the client gives their answers, stay aware and notice their tone of voice, body language and any shifts, pauses, uncertainties and so on. Note these discreetly as you listen. After this process, which can take between five and ten minutes, tell the client that you are now going to pause the conversation between them and Jane and spend a few minutes looking at what comes up for them in a quick process like this.

Who is in Charge of Who? Conversations with a Mobile Phone

4. In this next period, explore and be curious about the shifts and things you noticed during the conversation. Coach them to explore what they have noticed about the relationship with their phone. Ask them if there are echoes of this in respect to other technology devices they may own and use. Ask them what they notice about the relationship with their phone overall and if there is anything they would like to change.

5. Now ask them if they would like to say anything to their phone directly. This may strike your client as odd and they may be reluctant to do so – which is, of course, fine. In that case, tell them the role play is over and ask them to turn off the phone and put it in their pocket. Remove the chair.

6. Often, a client will want to say something to close the conversation with the phone. It may be a request, such as "Please can you leave me alone sometimes" or "Thank you for helping me". Keep everything light and playful as this helps the client navigate the role play.

7. Finally, end the session by designing some homework with the client that comes out of their insight. If they have nothing specific, suggest a few possible enquiries, one of which they can select or use as a basis to design one for themselves. Revisit this in your next session.

Anthony Eldridge-Rogers is a coach, facilitator, author and speaker specialising in Recovery and Wellness Coaching and the Meaning Centred Coaching model he created.

Route to the Top

Ingredients

Paper and pen or whiteboard

Penned image of a mountain side

Description

There's a philosophy that we can't become truly successful in anything by focusing on everything, and that we run the risk of achieving less than we're capable of if we don't stick closely or true to our priorities. There's a potential opportunity cost every time our focus strays off course. Actions that aren't aligned with our goals have the potential to take our time and attention away from what really matters to us.

This tool encourages clients to think about all the separate activities they're engaged in and to reflect on those that help them towards their goal and those that are not contributing or, worse still, are getting in the way of their progress.

When does it work best?

This tool is effective when you have a client that struggles with prioritising an endless list of goals, projects and ideas, and who wants help in re-evaluating their priorities in everyday life, at work or when events or circumstances change.

It can be useful for clients who feel they say yes too often and who, as a result, put themselves under pressure, take themselves off their own course and are left with a sense of having achieved nothing.

The technique will help clients to create more focus on their own goals and identify the individual activities that have the potential to propel them towards these goals.

Step by step

1. Create a picture of the goal together by asking your client to brainstorm all their 'ideals' around their goals, projects and ideas. The 'Magic Wand' question can be useful here or Michael Bungay Stanier's AWE question ("And what else?"). Often, there are more ideals than they initially thought. These can be personal or work related, or both.
2. Review the list together and ask them to nominate the five that are most important and meaningful to them to achieve. Ask them to put each of these on separate pieces of paper and lay them out in front of themselves.
3. Then ask them if the goals are serving one common, meaningful, high-level goal that they really do want to pursue. Ask them to try defining what that upper goal is and then how any of their top-five topics/goals relate to that.

If your client doesn't have one common, high-level goal, suggest to them that they consider choosing one. If they can't or don't want to – and this is often the case – you can discuss with them that this is OK, and how this might mean that they move forward at a slower pace overall but potentially achieve multiple things, albeit at this slower pace. This can be common and is often what I call a 'Ping' – a lightbulb moment – with clients who have multiple passions.

4. Ask them to look at the goals that are left on their list (i.e. not in the top five) and ask them if any of these contribute in any way to the upper goal(s). This will help them to see how their goals line up and support each other – or otherwise.

5. Now work with them to create order and priorities. Ask them to look again at the goals and explore with them how the goals build on each other. Ask them what needs to happen first so something else can move forward. Place these on the timeline where they belong (i.e. at the lower levels of the mountain). This is a good opportunity to explore how much time the client has available to achieve these items and to consider the impact.

    At this stage, your client should be encouraged to decide where to focus first and if there are items to put on hold for now. This can help the client to let go of trying to achieve too many items/goals at once.

6. Now look at the items and goals that are left. These are the items that your client should avoid working on completely. Discuss this with them and ask how they feel about ignoring these and how they might go about achieving that.

7. As a final step, you can work with your client to devise a way of helping them decide which goals to attend to and which to place on the back burner by co-creating some questions they could reliably use to help them to qualify their weekly or daily activities as 'in' or 'out'.

Maggie Grieve is an accredited leadership and team development coach, consultant and facilitator with 30 years of working with organisations and leaders across the world. She owns her own business, Ping Thinking, and is an external coach for NHS England.

Random Object

Ingredients

A bag or container with 12–24 small random objects

Description

This is a variant of the Random Word Selection/Word Search tool. Rather than selecting a word from a picture dictionary or book, the client is offered a selection of random objects from which to select (at random) as a means of helping them find a new way of approaching a problem and changing their perspective.

When does it work best?

It works well with a topic that has already been explored, without an obvious way forward having been identified. The tool encourages creative thought generated from random visual stimuli that may provoke a different way of thinking about things, generating new options.

Step by step

1. After allowing some silence and getting some signal that the client is struggling, offer to try an exercise that might help.
2. If they say yes, then explain that it involves using a bag with random objects. Reinforce the importance of a non-judgemental environment and focusing on quantity of ideas rather than quality.
3. Invite the client to put their hand in the bag and to select an object.
4. Provide the client with some space to consider the object. Follow up with a set of open questions, such as "How could this item be used to think about your topic?" or "In what way can you bring this object into the discussion about the current situation?"
5. Close the exercise with reflective questions, such as "What thoughts emerges for you as you reflect on this object?" or "How can this object be used to enable you to move forward one step towards your goal?"

Reference

Van Niewerburgh, C. (2014) *An Introduction to Coaching Skills: A Practical Guide*. London: Sage.

Claudia Day is a coach and entrepreneur, co-founder of My Coaching Place, part of the AC UK leadership team, and holds a master's in coaching and behavioural change (Henley) and a master's in business administration (MIT).

The Goal Pyramid: A Coaching Tool for Achieving Your Objectives

Ingredients

None

When does it work best?

The Goal Pyramid works best for individuals who want to achieve specific, measurable objectives. It is especially useful for long-term goals that may seem overwhelming or difficult to achieve. By breaking these goals down into smaller, more achievable steps, individuals can make steady progress towards their ultimate objective and maintain motivation along the way.

Description

The Goal Pyramid is a powerful coaching tool that helps individuals to set and achieve their goals by breaking them down into smaller, more manageable tasks. The pyramid structure provides a visual representation of the steps required to reach a specific objective and helps individuals to prioritise their actions and focus their efforts.

Step by step

1. Invite the client to identify a *dream goal*. Start by defining the ultimate objective. What do they want to achieve and by when?
2. Once they have identified their *dream goal*, invite them to break it down into *end goals*, or smaller, more specific objectives that they can achieve within a few months to a year.
3. Next, break each *end goal* down into even smaller, more achievable *performance*, or short-term, goals that they can accomplish within a few weeks to a few months. These should be quality-focused goals.
4. For each short-term goal, identify the specific *process goals* or actions that they need to take to achieve it. What steps do they need to follow and what resources do they need?
5. Finally, create a timeline for each short-term goal, including deadlines and milestones along the way. This will help them to stay on track and monitor progress. By combining the Goal Pyramid with the SMART goal framework, individuals can create a comprehensive and actionable plan for achieving their objectives. The pyramid structure provides a visual representation of the steps required to reach the ultimate goal, while the SMART criteria help to ensure that each task is specific, measurable, achievable, relevant and time-bound.

References

Doran, G.T. (1981) There's a SMART Way to Write Management's Goals and Objectives. *Management Review*, 70(11): 35–36.

Grant, A.M. (2003) The Impact of Life Coaching on Goal Attainment, Metacognition and Mental Health. *Social Behavior and Personality: An International Journal*, 31(3): 253–263.

Locke, E.A., and Latham, G.P. (2002) Building a Practically Useful Theory of Goal Setting and Task Motivation: A 35-Year Odyssey. *American Psychologist*, 57(9): 705–717.

Callum O'Neill is a BPS registered psychologist and ICF accredited coach (PCC).

Cynefin Framework

Ingredients

A pre-prepared graphic of the framework

Description

The Cynefin Framework is a useful tool to help decision-making in today's challenging world and has its origins in complexity science. The framework was created by Dave Snowden (Snowden and Boone, 2007) and is named after the Welsh word for 'habitat' (*cynefin*), which relates to the multiple factors in our environment that influence us.

The framework consists of five domains or decision-making contexts in which a client may perceive that they find themselves. These are *clear*, *complicated*, *complex*, *chaotic* and *confusion*. As time goes by and teams or organisations change, situations may move from one domain to the next, so what was originally a clear situation may become complicated.

- **Clear:** A clear (or simple) context that the client may be in is likely to be stable, with cause-and-effect relationships or best practice fairly obvious. It is an environment of 'known knowns' where rules or standard operating procedures are likely to be in place – if a client does A, then B happens in a pretty predictable manner. There is, however, a danger of over-simplification or complacency in this context and practices may get stuck in the past. The framework recommends a 'sense–categorise–respond' approach in such situations.
- **Complicated:** A complicated domain for a client exists where there are 'known unknowns', cause and effect may need some analytical work and there could be a range of solutions to problems or tasks. The recommended approach in this environment is to sense, then analyse, then respond.
- **Complex:** The complex situation is one full of 'unknown unknowns' where there may be no right answers and cause/effect is not clear until much later. The framework suggests a 'probe–sense–respond' approach, experimenting, especially where safe to do so.
- **Chaotic:** A chaotic environment is where immediate action, almost any action, is required by the leader to try to bring order. The framework recommends acting to establish order, then sensing to identify where stability may lie and then responding in order to turn the chaotic into the complex. A quick and decisive use of instinct may well be the first step in such situations, perhaps trying something new.
- **Confusion:** The confusion domain sits in the middle of all and indicates that the situation is so unclear that it cannot be categorised into one of the other four domains. Instead, the framework suggests breaking the situation down into constituent parts that can be viewed through one of the other four lenses.

Step by step

1. Orientate the client to the framework using a diagram to explain how it helps to categorise situations and suggests an approach to take in each domain.
2. Allow the client to reflect on their situation.
3. Explore how the framework may help bring a sense of perspective for the client.
4. Invite the client to generate ideas about possible options for action as a result of the newly gained perspectives.
5. Invite the client to use the framework in their workplace for discussion with others or for their own reflection.

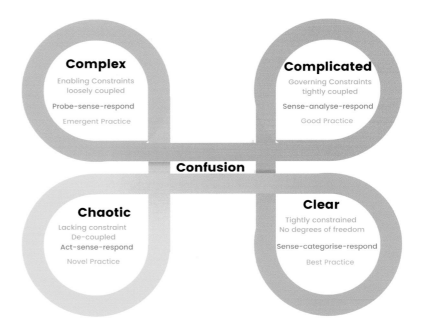

Reference

Snowden, D.J., and Boone, M.E. (2007) A Leader's Framework for Decision Making. *Harvard Business Review*, 85(11): 68.

Dave Crome is an accredited coach, consultant and Action-Centred Leadership trainer.

Visualisations: Coping Visualisation and Success Visualisation

Ingredients

None

When does it work best?

This technique works best for individuals preparing for important, high-stress events or situations. This might include a job interview, a presentation or a pitch to a key client. When high-pressure situations emerge, individual performance can be inhibited by unhelpful thoughts or catastrophising. These build anxiety and, in the moment, can interfere with performance. By preparing in advance through using these tools, client anxiety can be reduced and performance enhanced.

Description

Visualisation techniques are grounded in cognitive behavioural coaching and are widely used by elite athletes and others both to help prepare for challenging situations (coping visualisations) and also to build towards successful outcomes (success visualisation). In a coping visualisation, the client imagines themself in the difficult situation, what is happening and what they are feeling. The client then works through with their coach how they would want to respond: how they would wish to feel, think and behave. By preparing in this way, prior to an event, the individual can have at their disposal a plan to implement. In a success visualisation, a similar plan is followed, this time imagining the desired outcome. What is the best, ten-out-of-ten outcome? The client can then prepare by exploring what the factors were that led to this. How did they need to think, feel and behave to enable them to achieve this outcome?

Step by step

Option A: Coping visualisation

1. The coach invites the client to describe the situation and talk about their thoughts leading into the key event.
2. The coach then invites the client to imagine their feels being realised. What would be happening? How would they be feeling?
3. The coach can invite the client to make a written note of aspects that cause them the greatest anxiety.
4. Once the situation feels real, the coach can invite the client to move into slow-motion mode and to consider: How would they like to feel, think and behave? What could they do to reduce the feelings or anxiety? What could they do to feel more positive after the event? How could they behave to minimise the negative outcomes?
5. The coach can invite the client to make some notes from the insights, following this discussion, on possible actions.
6. The coach can then invite the client to repeat the visualisation but this time to employ the ideas and actions to minimise the impact of the events and their feelings about them.
7. At the close of the second visualisation, the coach can encourage a reflection about what has changed. Invite the client to write down a plan and reflect on any other insights they could action (if there are others or new ones, the coping visualisation can be repeated).

Option B: Success visualisation

1. The coach invites the client to describe the situation and talk about their thoughts leading into the key event.
2. The coach then invites the client to imagine the desired outcome, encouraging the client to make this as real as possible through adding how they will feel about the experience, and how others might react.
3. Once imagined, the coach invites the client to replay the scene, often going back before the scene started to understand what led to this desired outcome. How did the client prepare, what did they do, how and when? What did the client feel and how did they ensure these feelings were in place? What other things contributed to that outcome? The more detail the better.
4. Once this reflection has been discussed, the coach can invite the client to make some notes on the insights.
5. Finally, once they have developed this visualisation, it often helps clients if they are invited to replay this time and again leading into the event.

From experience, with key events, I have found it best to help clients to prepare both for the desired outcome but also for the plan not going as they'd hoped.

Jonathan Passmore is a chartered psychologist, accredited master coach, team coach, supervisor, author and professor at Henley Business School.

Leadership Logics

Ingredients

A leadership culture diagram

Description

Leadership Logics provides a way of exploring a client and/or their team's mindset to help improve their leadership capability and/or organisational culture. It builds on research regarding action logics (Torbert and Rooke, 2005), which explain how the development of an individual leader's thinking impacts their behaviour and actions.

Leadership Logics affects the type of culture a leadership team are collectively able to develop (McGuire and Palus, 1994) and indicates where their current boundaries in thinking may be. Understanding the various action logics can help a coach to better support coaching outcomes, personal growth and cultural development within organisations.

Leadership Cultures

Dependent	<<transition>>	Independent	<<transition>>	Interdependent
Responsibility for leadership sits with those in authority		The drive for achievement and individual ability cause leadership to emerge		Leadership is seen as a collective activity

Leadership (Action) Logics

Opportunistic	Diplomatic	Expertise	Achieving	Redefining	Transforming	Alchemical
Win for self in any way possible	Desire to belong and fit in	Focus on logic and expertise	Driven by both personal and team achievement	Unique reframing of complex problems	Generation of organisational and personal transformation	Integrates material, spiritual, and societal transformations

Increasing capacity to create and maintain shared direction, alignment, and commitment in the face of complexity and change →

Step by step

1. Explain the framework to the client in the coaching session or, in the case of a team, a workshop.
2. Invite the client(s) to position themselves and their organisation within the leadership culture diagram (for workshops, you may want to create a floor map or have a large version pinned to the wall).
3. Use your understanding of the various leadership logics to question, probe and clarify the position they have identified.
4. Ask where they and their team need to be to achieve success, and why this is so.
5. Use your understanding of the various leadership logics to question, probe and clarify that position.

6. For teams, at this point you will need to facilitate a discussion to reach a place of agreement or actions to reach a place of agreement. If the latter is likely, split this into two or more sessions.
7. Use visualisation or another technique to solidify that goal.
8. Agree appropriate coaching interventions to reach that goal.

When does it work best?

The technique works best when a client is beginning to recognise that either their own way of thinking doesn't work or that the thinking of their team seems to be more limited than is desired. For an individual, this can appear as a contradiction in what they recognise is needed by others (i.e. their emotional intelligence and their own behaviour or thinking are at odds with what others need, for example: "how could I agree? It would put me at risk!"). For a leader and their team, this can surface through comments such as "they don't get it" and often occurs when they are leading change.

Important considerations prior to using the model are:
- Is the client open to the fact that they may need to change their own thinking or behaviour? If not, this tool may raise awareness but deeper work is not recommended.
- Are they willing to put the effort in to expand their own thinking? This process requires what can be challenging conversations or exercises and may not be comfortable.
- How comfortable are you in your mutual ability to realistically assess where the individual or team are currently working within this framework? If you are not where you need to be, what additional information might help? Do you need 360° feedback?

References

McGuire, J.B., and Palus, C.J. (1994) Vertical Transformation of Leadership Culture. *Integral Review*, 41: 144–166.

Torbert, W.R., and Rooke, D. (2005) Seven Transformations of Leadership. *Harvard Business Review*, April.

Note: The diagram for this tool was produced by Christine Lithgow Smith.

Christine Lithgow Smith is a doctoral candidate specialising in leadership awareness, an accredited coach and managing director at Chrisalyst Ltd.

Tweet

Ingredients

Phone, tablet (e.g. iPad) or paper

Maggie Grieve is an accredited leadership and team development coach, consultant and facilitator with 30 years of working with organisations and leaders across the world. She owns her own business, Ping Thinking, and is also an external coach for NHS England.

Description

This is a technique that uses the Twitter concept of a limit on words to help a client describe a coaching topic or scenario. Its aim is to encourage a client to articulate, quickly and concisely, the real heart of their topic or goal in a coaching conversation. The idea is that the client is able to use the 280-character limit of Twitter to distil their issue to a focussed idea.

Step by step

1. Invite the client to create a Twitter message that explains their current situation or challenge. (You can suggest the previous Twitter limit of 140 characters or you could extend this to the current limit of 280 characters, if necessary. It can also be helpful to explain the concept, but give your client a number of words as a limit rather than characters.)
2. Confirm to them that they must stay within the character limit (140 or 280) or word limit (perhaps 20).
3. If desired, and to get the creative flow going, you could show some good examples of tweets on other subjects that convey a lot of information in very few words or ask them to find a great example themselves to share.
4. Use the tweet created by the client to discuss the topic more fully.

Time Management Matrix

Ingredients

Paper

Pen or pencil

Description

The Time Management Matrix is a tool that helps a client to categorise their activities or the tasks on their to-do list by level of importance and urgency, and therefore gain clarity on where they currently focus their time and effort. This leads to a conversation about where the client would prefer to spend their energy and allows them to make deliberate choices about the activities to which they pay attention. As described by Stephen Covey (2004), each activity is added to one of four quadrants:

I. **Important and Urgent**: Tasks with an upcoming deadline, unexpected crises, pressing issues

II. **Important and Not Urgent**: Planning, reflection, creative idea generation, relationship building, recreation
(Covey suggests that these activities have the greatest impact, but are often overlooked in favour of urgent activities.)

III. **Not Important and Urgent**: Interruptions, some phone calls and emails, some meetings

IV. **Not Important and Not Urgent**: Some phone calls and emails, some meetings, 'busy' work

There are numerous visuals of Covey's Four Quadrant matrix available on the internet and the most appropriate version can be selected and shared with the client.

Step by step

1. Introduce the tool, explaining that it is a time-management tool to sort activities, projects or tasks into four quadrants based on their level of importance and urgency. It is helpful to share a visual that describes the type of activities that will generally fall into each quadrant, as well as the outcomes of focusing in respective quadrants.

2. Invite the client to draw two intersecting lines dividing a piece of paper into four quadrants. Write "Urgent" at the top of the left column and "Not Urgent" at the top of the right column. Label the top row "Important" and the second row "Not Important".

Time Management Matrix

	URGENT	NOT URGENT
IMPORTANT	I	II
NOT IMPORTANT	III	IV

3. Next, ask the client to list their activities or tasks and add each one to the appropriate quadrant based on its importance and urgency.
4. You might ask the client to describe why they added a particular task into a specific quadrant. For example, if task X has been added in the "Important" row, you could ask "How does task X help you to achieve your strategic objectives?"
5. Ask "And what else?" to allow the client to articulate their activities fully.
6. Once the client is satisfied that they have a comprehensive overview, ask them to quantify the percentage of their time spent on tasks in each quadrant, using a question such as "In an average week, what proportion of time do you spend on Quadrant I activities?"
7. Next, ask what strikes them about the amount of time spent. The client's insights about how they manage and spend their time lead to a conversation about where they would like to expend their efforts, and what they need to say no to in order to make the shift towards the highly impactful activities of Quadrant II.

Reference

Covey, S.R. (2004) *The 7 Habits of Highly Effective People: Powerful Lessons in Personal Change.* London: Simon & Schuster UK Ltd.

Sarah Gledhill is an accredited coach who specialises in the higher education and non-profit sectors, following an international fundraising career.

Dreamer

Ingredients

Pen and paper

Description

This exercise challenges the client to allow themselves to dream on a daily basis. The objective is for the client to name three dreams for the day, whether they are small or big. This exercise helps to prioritise the client's goals.

Step by step

1. Invite the client, if they are willing, to try an experiment and explain why you have considered using this exercise.
2. Ask the client to outline three things they dream of, providing examples that relate to their context or yours if necessary (e.g. "I dream of having a nice family day", "I dream I will make a sale", "I dream I will feel energetic", "I dream that this week will be fun and go quickly").
3. Ask the client how they feel about the exercise and explore these feelings to understand if they are supportive of it.
4. Invite the client to journal three-to-five dreams on a daily basis, deciding on the frequency based on the client's preference.
5. Help the client to find a way to merge this activity with another routine activity to make it easier to remember to do it.
6. Identify potential obstacles and plan for them.
7. Continue coaching as usual.

When does it work best?

This exercise works best for clients who have given up without trying or those who are dissatisfied with several aspects of their life but are hesitant to change.

Reference

Robbins, M. (Host). (2022, November 10). Your Dreams Are NO Joke: It's Time to DREAM BIG Again (No. 86) [Audio podcast episode]. In *The Mel Robbins Podcast*.

Claudia Day is a coach and entrepreneur, co-founder of My Coaching Place, part of the AC UK leadership team, and holds a master's in coaching and behavioural change (Henley) and a master's in business administration (MIT).

The Question Swap

Ingredients

None

Description

Rapid advances in technology continue to accelerate change at unprecedented speeds. Quite simply, the pace of change is faster than it has ever been and it will never be this slow again. Add to this the incredible amount of volatility and uncertainty we have and continue to experience worldwide. Now more than ever, this requires leaders to make rapid decisions. Thus, it is no surprise that leaders at all levels are under a tremendous amount of pressure to perform. This pressure can drive impatience and frustration, leading to counterproductive behaviours, particularly when it comes to high-stakes conversations driven by a naturally reactive leader (what Robert Hogan refers to as "excitable").

Naturally reactive or excitable leaders under duress can be particularly counter-productive in their conversations. Their reactivity can put the other person into a defensive posture, shifting the conversation into a more adversarial exchange. Add to this the power dynamic of a superior–subordinate relationship and you have a recipe for derailment. A technique to help counter this is the Question Swap. The idea is to work with the client on replacing reactive statements with questions.

When does it work best?

This technique works best when you hear a client expressing challenges in communicating with team members where it appears that reactivity and emotional regulation are at play. The idea is to work with the client to recognise the circumstances where they may be inclined to unwittingly shut down healthy conversations by their reactive nature and understand what triggers those reactions.

The hope is that the question will help facilitate constructive dialogue. Sometimes the use of a question will help buy the client a little more time to redirect the negative energy of their initial reaction towards a more neutral state of mind. This can allow them to get to a better mental space where they are more open to hearing out the other person.

Step by step

1. Work with your client to identify the circumstances (types of meetings, particular individuals, etc.) as well as specific triggers (words, behaviours, etc.) that lead to their negative reactivity.
2. Help them identify the physical cues in themselves that may indicate they are about to react (raised blood pressure, elevated stress, etc.).
3. Discus experimenting with using this leading indicator as a prompt to

The Question Swap

pause, so as to allow them time to recognise they have been triggered in the moment.

4. Prepare the question swap. Here you will work with the client on identifying questions they can use to replace what would otherwise be a negative derailing statement. The idea is first to pause and then to insert a question instead of a statement. Consider using the following categories of questions that I refer to as your 'question DEC' (define, elaborate or clarify).

   a. So, what do you specifically mean when you say XYZ?

   b. Can you elaborate or provide more detail on that?

   c. Can you clarify what you are proposing? What will this look like? Instead of reacting or attacking, the client is now encouraging deeper thought through probing. This can keep the dialogue going and put the onus of the conversation on the other individual while your client collects themselves so as to re-engage in a healthy way. Work with your client to select a specific upcoming one-on-one or meeting at which they can try the technique – and get them to commit to the experiment.

5. Review how it went at your next session. Discuss what it felt like and explore how the other individual reacted differently than in past conversations where Question Swap was not used.

References

Carver, C.S., and Scheier, M.F. (1998) *On the Self-regulation of Behavior.* New York: Cambridge University Press.

Hogan, R., Kaiser, R.B., Sherman, R.A., and Harms, P.D. (2021) Twenty Years on the Dark Side: Six Lessons about Bad Leadership. *Consulting Psychology Journal: Practice and Research*, 73(3): 199–213.

Dr Woody Woodward is Clinical Assistant Professor of Executive Coaching at New York University School of Professional Studies.

Producer–product Balance for Productivity on Healthy Terms

Ingredients

Flipchart

Markers

Pen and paper

Description

What came first, the egg or the chicken? Who cares! Both are key and interdependent. One thing is certain: healthy chickens lay good eggs. A vital aspect of healthy balance that is often forgotten is the balance between you the producer (or your team if you work with others) and the products or results you're delivering – the egg. By not paying attention to this balance, it is easy to exhaust the producer and sabotage results, if not in the short term then certainly over the long term.

Think of wellbeing, health and sustainable productivity as a multiple of two numbers: the health and wellbeing of the producer and the product. If the producer is tired or weak, the overall result will be less than what you or your team is capable of.

A vital part of healthy productivity and balance is taking care of the producer – *you*. When your needs are met, you'll be in a good place to perform at your best in life and at work. Healthy productivity is sustainable. You deliver results without wearing yourself down. In fact, it's worth considering how you can deliver results and feel renewed by the process.

While most people are familiar with the concept of crunch times, for some people work can be a constant series of high-octane work until they burn out. The danger with spending all or most of your energy on producing results (eggs) is that at some point you – the producer (hen) – become exhausted. Wellbeing and joy plummet, and chronic stress ensues.

The Producer–product Balance is a simple coaching exercise to support healthy balance and was inspired by the medical triage system. It can be used to support you as a coach and to coach other individuals and/or teams towards healthy balance. The activity takes little time while developing critical awareness of how things are on two fronts – the producer and the product – and how to manage and show up to the needs of both. It will easily pinpoint areas that may require minor or major tweaks and/or acknowledge where healthy balance already exists.

When does it work best?

This activity works well:
- At the start of a coaching session, as a way to quickly check in
- As a more in-depth exercise to explore wellbeing and productivity
- To help focus effort and energy
- For exploring healthy balance in different settings: team leader/team with results, supplier with distributor, company/associates with client delivery, etc.
- For shifting from stress to productive action
- For developing self-compassion
- For team check-in or an away-day activity
- For product-development coaching
- For business-development coaching.

Step by step

1. **Set up**: Invite your client to imagine themselves or their team as a healthy hen that produces a healthy stream of eggs. For personal or life coaching, the eggs could represent, for example, health, family, job, career or fulfilling relationships. For executive coaching, the eggs can stand for a successful project, a fruitful collaboration or a well-functioning team. The healthy chicken is you – the maker, doer, leader, producer. Invite your client to focus inwards on themselves as this producer who is in top mental, emotional, physical and spiritual form. In other words, at their best.

2. **Ranking**: Draw the following table on a flipchart and explain the five categories.

   Top health – excellent condition
   So-so – there is room to improve
   Sickly – you know what's wrong and how to fix it
   Critical – needs attention now
   Dead – completely exhausted or lost

   Invite your client to rank their current health state as the producer (the hen) and each of their key products (eggs) using the scale provided. Here are possible coaching questions:
   - Where do you think/feel you fit best along this scale as the producer?
   - What is it like to be here for you?
   - Bring to mind one of your key products/services and notice where it fits best at the moment.
   - What are you basing this decision on?
   - Note where the key focus is right now – on the product or producer?
   - What's needed to create health, wellbeing and a sustainable way forward?

	Top health	So-so	Sickly	Critical	Dead
Producer					
Product 1					
Product 2					

3. **Awareness building and envisaging a better future for the producer(s)**: Invite your client to pick a box representing where they are today as the producer. You may also want to explore with your client where they would place themselves last year or three years ago. This is a helpful indicator for your client as to whether things are staying the same, getting worse or improving. Then, invite your client to tell you where they would like to be in 12 months or three years. Is this realistic? What may need to change or shift within their habitual way of being and operating? If they lead a team, you can also add another row for the team as a whole or rows for each team member.

	Top health	So-so	Sickly	Critical	Dead
Producer		√			
Product 1					
Product 2					

4. **Awareness building and envisaging a better future for the products**: Ask them to rate their main product(s). If they have more than one, as many clients often do, simply include more fields. You may want to help your client to clarify the relative priority and state of completion of each.

	Top health	So-so	Sickly	Critical	Dead
Producer		√			
Product 1	√				
Product 2				√	

5. **Noticing and evidencing the whole picture**: Invite the client to notice what the emerging picture says about the current balance, health and needs of their system. What evidence do they have and what may be missing. What do they need to discover or find out more about? What assumptions are they making that may be skewing the balance for them? This will help you both validate and explore the picture in greater depth and lead to natural problem solving.

6. **Goal setting and action taking**: Invite the person to name one or two actions that would most improve on the current situation. Think about short- and mid-term time scales and ways of marking progress to sustain motivation for the client. You may also want to explore the best ways you as coach could support and hold the client accountable.

Reference

Bak-Maier, M. (2012) *Get Productive! Boosting Your Productivity and Getting Things Done.* Capstone.

Dr Magdalena Bak-Maier is an international teacher and coach trainer who helps people reconnect with their full potential.

Career Highs and Lows

Ingredients

Sheet of paper

Pen or pencil

Description

Career Highs and Lows is a tool to help the client reflect on their career path and its peaks and troughs. It facilitates a review of jobs, which are plotted on a timeline from earliest to most recent, noting down what made each fulfilling, what aspects were less rewarding and the lessons learned throughout the career journey. The client can then identify themes across their career and gain insights on what may be missing in their current role or help to decide on a future direction.

When does it work best?

Career Highs and Lows is a great tool to use when a client is at a career cross-roads and unsure about next steps. It is also good for a client who is feeling stuck, lacks motivation or is dissatisfied with their current role or work. The tool helps the client to reflect on their career path and the elements of each job that were personally rewarding and those that were less fulfilling. The clarity that is gained enables a conversation about moving towards a desired objective. It can also help the client to shift their attention away from the current role to reflect on successes throughout their career and learnings at each stage. This is useful for a client who is having a crisis of confidence due to a current work situation. The tool can be used either during a coaching conversation or as a reflective exercise by the client outside of the session, followed by a discussion about the insights gained.

Step by step

1. Explain the tool to the client.
2. If you agree to work together to explore career highs and lows during a coaching session, ask the client to draw a horizonal timeline across the middle of a piece of paper (landscape works best), with year of first job on the far left and current year on the far right.
3. Ask the client to add their jobs to the timeline in chronological order, along with the associated dates. Include early roles such as casual work, although multiple similar such roles can be grouped together.
4. Then, starting with the first role, ask the client what they liked and disliked about the job and to write down positives above the line and negatives below the line. Clients can sometimes feel uncomfortable talking about their first few jobs, but drawing out what they enjoyed or found difficult in early roles can be quite illuminating.
5. Once the first job has been explored, ask about the next role.

Step by step

1. Give a brief overview of PIES and seek the client's permission to use it.
2. Initially, ask the client to indicate where they are on a scale of 1–10 against each element.
3. If using the tool as a check-in, ask them if there is anything that they notice as they share their assessment or if there is anything that needs attention in the coaching session today; or is there anything they need/want from you the coach in the session? (This can help the client identify how much challenge/support they may want.)
4. If using the tool for further work on resilience or self-awareness, you can take each element in turn, or ask the client whether there is one element in particular they wish to think about or that would be valuable to work on. You can then explore using multiple questions. The following are just a few examples, as there are so many options:
   a. How do you know you are at a particular point on the scale of 1–10?
   b. What has enabled you to be at this level?
   c. What resources have you utilised to be there?
   d. What might/do you want to change?
   e. Where would you be on the scale if you made this change?
   f. What might you do to move up a notch?
   g. How would that be?

Julia Carden is an accredited coach and coach supervisor, and a visiting tutor at Henley Business School.

Elephant, Dead Fish and Vomit

Ingredients

Paper and pens
(optional)

When does it work best?

This exercise helps clients go deeper with any issue that they are struggling with, particularly where the issue concerns a team or group that they are working in. Whilst it can be used in one-to-one coaching, it works particularly well in team coaching and can be used as a way to give individuals permission to voice something that would otherwise remain unsaid.

Reference

Morgan, B. (2017) *How to Build the Most Customer Focused Culture in the World.* Available from: https://www.forbes.com/sites/blakemorgan/2017/12/11/how-to-build-the-most-customer-focused-culture-in-the-world [Retrieved 4 May 2023].

Claire Rason is a coach, the founder of professional services, coaching-powered consultancy Client Talk and host of the podcast Lawyer's Coach.

Description

Everyone has heard the metaphor of the elephant in the room. This tool extends that metaphor and helps clients explore issues differently. This tool is widely credited as having helped Airbnb build a strong company culture by helping open up internal dialogue (Morgan, 2017). However, when used as a coaching tool, it can help clients voice things that would usually go unsaid and view problems from different perspectives. When used in team coaching, this exercise can help build psychological safety.

Step by step

1. If you are working with a team, start by contracting with them. This exercise might reveal things that are normally hidden. What does each team member need from others in the team to get the most from the exercise? What are the rules that the team will be bound by?
2. Start by inviting the client (if one to one) or the group (if team) to consider what 'the elephant in the room' is for the issue they are stuck on. Explain that this is something that everyone knows, but that nobody wants to discuss. Like an elephant would be in a room, it is hard to ignore.
3. If you are doing this in a team, you might want to invite everyone to write down what they think the elephant is on a piece of paper. Get them to put their piece of paper on the ground/table and then get everyone to pick up someone else's paper. Go around the room and read out the elephants that have been identified. Doing it this way can make it easier for people to share.
4. Explore the elephant with your client(s). Think about why the elephant isn't acknowledged. How can the elephant be made visible? What does the elephant's invisibility mean for the wider issue that is being explored? If in a team, how many people identified the same elephant? Was anyone surprised by what came out?
5. The next step is to explain dead fish. These are things that died in the past, but they are still rotting. They have an impact. Are there any dead fish with regards to the issue at hand? Again, if working in a team, you can invite members to write thoughts on paper and get people to read someone else's response.
6. Explore what has come out. Maybe there weren't any dead fish. What does that mean for this issue? What is in the past of this team/organisation?
7. Finally, explore the concept of vomit. What is the thing that you are wanting to say but don't feel able to. Maybe it is something that is obvious to you and so you don't feel it is worth saying. Again, if in teams, you can use the paper exercise to gather everyone's thoughts.
8. Reflect on what has come to light. What does having the elephant, fish and vomit out in the open mean for the issue at hand?

The Quicksand Anxiety Metaphor

Ingredients

Pen and paper

When does it work best?

This technique works best for helping clients who are feeling low or who are consumed by worries or anxiety. However, in cases where clients are experiencing suicidal thoughts or may be clinically depressed, the coach should refer the client to a medical doctor.

Reference

Stoddard, J.A., and Afari, N. (2014) *The Big Book of ACT Metaphors: A Practitioner's Guide to Experiential Exercises and Metaphors in Acceptance and Commitment Therapy*. Oakland, CA: New Harbinger Publications.

Jonathan Passmore is a chartered psychologist, accredited master coach, team coach, supervisor, author and professor at Henley Business School.

Description

Metaphor is a frequently used tool in coaching, with different metaphors serving different purposes. In this case, the metaphor is drawn from acceptance and commitment therapy (Stoddard and Afari, 2014), but adapted for use in workplace coaching and with clients who may be feeling overwhelmed or experiencing high stress levels. The metaphor involves an imagined scenario of being trapped in quicksand. Without making the explicit link, the coach is directing the client to consider in which ways their anxiety or worries are like quicksand; for example, the more they struggle, the deeper they sink. In contrast, the more they 'lay back' and accept their situation, the more opportunity or time there is for escape or rescue.

Step by step

1. The coach invites the client to consider the following scenario: "Imagine you are walking in the desert. Suddenly, you step in quicksand and begin to sink rapidly. What do you do now?"
2. The coach can follow this with "What happens as you try to escape the quicksand?" or "What are the thoughts that come to your mind as you keep sinking?"
3. After an exploration of this hypothetical situation, the coach can invite the client to consider their current situation. For instance, "What do you do when you start sinking into your anxiety/worries?"
4. It works best for the coach not to make an explicit comparison between struggling with quicksand and struggling with anxiety or worries. Instead, allow the client to make this comparison in a way that fits their world.
5. The coach can facilitate the conversation, helping the client towards identifying some actions that reduce their anxiety by creating a focus on survival as opposed to multiple actions generated by panic.

Fostering Eureka! Moments

Ingredients

None

When does it work best?

In addition to using these questions when a person is showing symptoms of stress during coaching, they can be used for check-ins to ensure that the client activates the brain state that allows them to learn and which makes them most resourceful for the coaching session.

Description

'Eureka!' moments are frequently mentioned by clients and coaches as some of the most impressive and rewarding outcomes of coaching: the breakthrough moments when a problem one has been pondering on, and which has been consuming energy and focus for a long time, suddenly vanishes and feelings of relief and progress appear. Additional excitement comes from the fact that these 'eureka!' moments appear unexpectedly: under the shower, half asleep on the commuter train or in other mundane situations.

This surprise nature of 'eureka!' moments may leave one thinking they cannot be controlled. However, neuroscientific research shows that a coach can actively create an environment that increases the likelihood of the client having more 'eureka!' moments. This is achieved by deactivating the brain's task-positive network and activating its default-mode network by tapping into memories or asking them for a personal preference.

Step by step

1. Ask the client a question that requires them to tap into memories or make a personal judgement. For example:
   "What is your favourite ice-cream flavour?"
   "What did you like most about last year's holiday?"
   "What kind of drink do you like?"
   "What surprised you the most today?"
   "What are you looking forward to this weekend?"
   "What is your favourite animal?"
   "What is your favourite dish?"
   Usually, asking for a 'favourite' thing is best, because it both activates the default-mode network and sends the client on a positive trajectory.
2. Re-do step 1 whenever necessary.

Reference

Müller, F., and Greif, S. (2022) Insights through Coaching. In S. Greif, H. Möller, W. Scholl, J. Passmore and F. Müller (eds), *International Handbook of Evidence-Based Coaching*. Berlin: Springer. Available from:

Felix Müller is a business coach based in Germany, helping people in recognising and reaching professional goals.

Yes, and…

Ingredients

Optional: a ball or other object

Description

This is a tool borrowed from improvisational theatre and comedy. It is a way of thinking and interacting that focuses on accepting and building on 'offers' made by others ("yes, and"), rather than blocking suggestions ("yes, but"). The principle is that listening actively, being open to new ideas and not judging our own or others' suggestions can lead to more constructive and collaborative relationships and exciting new possibilities.

'Yes, and…' is a very flexible tool and there are a number of exercises that can be used in coaching sessions or as homework to help build skills around active listening, collaboration and supportive behaviours or to help promote creative problem solving and the generation of new ideas. It can also help clients with confidence and developing skills around spontaneity, thinking on their feet and flexibility of thinking.

Listen – expand without judgement – reflect

When does it work best?

This tool can work either as a way of building skills within individuals and teams or for the generation of specific new ideas – and often as both. It works well with clients who are open to experiential and creative approaches. However, everyone can learn from and enjoy 'Yes, and…'. It is important for the coach to emphasise that the technique is about experimentation in a safe environment. The coach should be willing to demonstrate and potentially take part in the exercise.

Step by step

Individual coaching:
1. Explain to the client that 'Yes, and…' is about freeing up their thinking and creativity, so the exercise will not be about saying the 'right' or 'best' thing but about listening and spontaneously responding.
2. Begin by asking what (fictitious) activity the client would like to plan with you – for example, a team away day or a holiday. The only rules are that they have to begin each suggestion with "Yes, and…", specifically building on the previous idea, and that the rules of the rational world do not apply. If they end up having the team Christmas party in space, so be it!
3. The coach should begin by saying "Let's…" followed by whatever activity the client wanted to plan – for example, "Let's go on a summer holiday". The client should respond with "yes, and let's…" followed by a specific suggestion.
4. Continue alternating with "Yes, and" suggestions until the activity seems to reach a natural conclusion or the energy wanes.
5. Encourage the client to reflect on these questions:
   • What surprised them about the exercise?
   • How did it feel to say "Yes, and…"?
   • How did it feel to be responded to using "Yes, and…" and to see their ideas develop?
   • Did they ever feel they were blocking the coach's suggestions or that they were being blocked?

- What did they find challenging about the exercise?
- How could the principles of 'Yes, and…' show up more in their life, their work or in relation to their goal? (This is an opportunity to identify specific actions and ideas, such as having 'Yes, and…' warm-ups in meetings.)

6. If the client would like to generate creative ideas in response to a specific issue or goal they have, they can repeat the process using a real-world suggestion and keeping the ideas more closely bounded by reality. However, they should avoid too much judgement or filtering. That can come later.

Group coaching:

1. In a group session of two or more people, everybody sits in a circle.
2. The coach starts with a short sentence that describes the goal and invites the member to their left to finish it. For example, if a couple is trying to get out of their routine on weekends, the coach could start with, "To make weekends more exciting we can start the day by…" and then signal to the group member to their left to finish the sentence.
   After they propose something, the member following says "Yes, and…" followed by something that builds on the previous suggestion until each idea is genuinely heard and developed. It is very important that this suggestion specifically builds on the previous suggestion, rather than simply being another thing that they could do at the weekend. So, if the suggestion is "Let's go swimming", the next suggestion could be "Yes, and let's try sea swimming at Whitstable" and so forth. So each idea is genuinely listened to and developed. If the idea has been fully developed, then another suggestion can be begun.
3. All the members repeat this process two or three times, depending on the time available and the energy in the round. If the energy is low, it may help to have a ball that indicates whose turn it is to talk, and the rounds can be done in a random order.
4. At the end of the exercise, the members reflect on how it went. How do they feel about the options that were offered? Which would they choose to try first and why?

Claudia Day is a coach and entrepreneur, co-founder of My Coaching Place, part of the AC UK leadership team, and holds a master's in coaching and behavioural change (Henley) and a master's in business adminis-tration (MIT).

Julie Flower is a leadership development coach, consultant and facilitator, with a specialism in improvi-sation in complex systems. She is also an external tutor in executive coaching at Henley Business School.

Timed Talk

Ingredients

A timer (a mobile phone can be used)

A coin

Description

Nancy Kline (1999) describes Timed Talk as "a way to have a fight in a Thinking Environment – or rather a way not to have a fight". Timed Talk keeps thinking and communication channels open in contentious situations or where a relationship roadblock has been reached. It helps clients to develop new ideas and work better together, in a comparatively quick time.

Using Timed Talk allows the people involved in a heated debate the opportunity to hear each other and start thinking, instead of just reacting, by providing each person in the discussion with the same time to talk and the same rules around talking. It often makes difficult things become easy.

When does it work best?

The principles of Timed Talk can be used in one-on-one scenarios, as well as in team scenarios to encourage whole team participation in a topic.

The technique works best where a leader, a team or an individual is involved in a situation where emotions are running high and decisions have therefore become difficult. Kline describes it as "turning cross-fire into creative cross-fire". The approach stops interruptions and the "loudest voice" from being the dominant or only voice, and it encourages creative solution-based thinking because everyone involved becomes confident that their voice will be heard. It is this that creates a way forward when there has previously been an impasse between individuals.

As well as being effective at breaking deadlock, Timed Talk also works well to establish the right environment for creativity and to progress ideas. It can thus be used very successfully during the planning phase of a new project or when looking for new ideas to explore.

Step by step

1. Gather the individuals or the team together.
2. Work with the participants to agree what the topic is that needs to be discussed. Examples I have worked with in the past include "she never pulls her weight so I end up doing everything", "sales don't care about the rest of us – they just keep selling stuff we can't support and shrug when we advise them of this" and "their proposed change to the process doesn't work for us".

Timed Talk

3. Spend some time describing the process you are about to follow: each person in the discussion will be provided with the same time to talk and the same rules around talking about the issue.
4. Outline and seek agreement to the principles/rules for participants:
    o   Focus on a team win or win–win, not individual wins
    o   Try to be truly fascinated by the speaker – they are brilliant!
    o   Listeners should smile and nod periodically.
5. The coach can flip a coin to decide who goes first.
6. The coach sets a timer for three minutes.
7. Each person has three minutes to share their perspective.
8. The other team members are asked to listen without interruption, and to give the speaker eye contact while they are talking.
9. Repeat until the issue is resolved.

Reference

Kline, N. (1999) *Time to Think: Listening to Ignite the Human Mind*. London: Cassell.

Maggie Grieve is an accredited leadership and team development coach, consultant and facilitator with 30 years of working with organisations and leaders across the world. She owns her own business, Ping Thinking, and is also an external coach for NHS England.

Practice Process and Purpose Worksheet

Ingredients

Paper and pens

When does it work best?

The tool works best as a precursor to developing or updating:
- Your coaching profile
- Your coaching contract.

Description

The Practice Process and Purpose Worksheet provides a format to help a coach reflect on how they communicate their coaching offer to potential clients. Clarifying the values, beliefs, experience, personal history and style preferences that inform your practice helps articulate the practice in a way that is congruent with who you are. This helps you create a 'golden thread' between your coaching contract, the way you establish and maintain coaching agreements for a session and the way your clients experience you.

Step by step

1. On a large sheet of paper, draw the three columns and head them 'Practice', 'Process' and 'Purpose' (see Table).
2. Start with Column 1: Practice. Use the questions as a catalyst to consider what informs your coaching offer and your coaching practice.
3. Next, move to Column 3: Purpose. How do these questions help you define your value proposition? What else do you need to ask yourself?
4. Then consider Column 2: Process. What insights have you gained from reflecting on your practice and purpose that will inform the way you work with clients? Use the questions to think about how you design the way you work and the process of your coaching programmes and sessions in a way that is congruent with your practice and purpose.
5. Step back – what would you say about the way you work?
6. Having completed this exercise, is there anything that needs to change to create a better alignment between your coaching profile, what you discuss with potential clients and your contracts and the way your clients experience you in practice?

Table: Practice Process and Purpose Template

Practice: What informs my coaching offer?	Process: How do I coach?	Purpose: What is the value of my coaching?
What is relevant from my: <ul><li>Life history</li><li>Coach education certification courses</li><li>Prior professional experience?</li></ul> What theories underpin my practice? What are my assumptions about human nature and how we can change? Who are the individuals who inspire me? What values and beliefs shape the way I work with clients?	What does a programme of coaching sessions look like? What tools, models, processes and techniques do I use? What is the shape of the individual session? How do I want to be with clients? How do I define my boundaries for coaching? How do I create the coaching relationship?	What is my intent? What difference do I want to make? What do my clients experience? What results do they get? What do my clients say about me? What changes happen? How do I measure success? What is the contribution to the wider system/context?

References

Jackson, P., and Bachkirova, T. (2019) The 3 Ps of Supervision and Coaching. In S. Palmer and E. Turner (eds), *The Heart of Coaching Supervision*, pp.20–41. New York, NY: Routledge.

Lane, D., Watts, M., and Corrie, S. (2016) *Supervision in the Psychological Professions: Building Your Own Personalised Model.* London: Open University Press.

Elizabeth Crosse is an ICF MCC, mentor, coach and supervisor. Her research and practice focus on coaches' continuous professional and personal development.

Tell Me about Yourself: Using Self-portraits in Coaching

Ingredients

Smartphone or camera

Printer (optional)

Client's self-portrait

When is it best to use it?

The technique can be used anytime during the coaching process, although it can be instrumental in the first session. As part of this session, we often start by saying to the client, "Tell me about yourself". Some clients feel comfortable, while others struggle. Furthermore, whichever is the case, using self-portraits will allow the client to go much deeper, connecting with ideas and parts of themselves they probably could not have previously considered.

Description

Those questions that seem the easiest to answer are often the most challenging. For example, the answer to "Who are you?" may need extensive introspection and reflection. Still, it is crucial to understand ourselves. Understanding our feelings, values and beliefs, and discovering our strengths and weaknesses, are actions of self-discovery and self-knowledge considered a critical ingredient for effective coaching. As Aristotle said, "Knowing ourselves is the beginning of all wisdom", and pursuing wisdom should be an endeavour in all coaching engagements.

The self-portrait, a picture of oneself as one sees it, has been a constant throughout the history of art and photography. The individual is the topic, the subject and the photograph's viewer. By taking photos of themselves, clients can discover who they are and could be, therefore connecting to their expectations (Weiser, 2018). In summary, this technique, and the adaptation of similar ones used in phototherapy and therapeutic photography, makes a case for using a self-portrait as a powerful resource to explore the self in coaching.

When using photography, as is the case with any other specific approach or technique, the coach will discuss this with the client during the chemistry session (the first time they meet with the client to decide if they will work together). If the client agrees, the coach will suggest that the self-portrait captures a positive quality or something they like about themselves. The client will also be encouraged to be creative and should understand that the picture can be as figurative or abstract as they want. The client will also decide if they want to include their face or not. Also, it is essential to make clear there is no correct or incorrect way to do a self-portrait. This may result in clients taking a picture of their whole body or part of it, or even focusing on a detail such as a tattoo or wrinkles.

Step by step

1. Ask your client to bring a self-portrait to their first session.
2. When appropriate during the session (for example, after contracting), ask the client to show the picture and introduce themselves by describing what they see in the self-portrait.
3. Encourage the client to keep talking by asking questions such as "And what else?"
4. If appropriate, ask other questions, such as "What are your best qualities?", "How do you think others see you?", "How would you like to

be seen?", "If you were to change something about yourself, what would it be?" Specific questions could be helpful to narrow the focus of a self-portrait.

5. Ask the client how the image of themselves they have described relates to their goal or primary desired outcome of the coaching.
6. Ask the client how the experience has been for them and what they have learnt about themselves that they did not know or were not conscious of before.

Reference

Weiser, J. (2018) *Phototherapy Techniques: Exploring the Secrets of Personal Snapshots and Family Albums.* Routledge.

Andrea Giraldez-Hayes is a chartered psychologist, accredited coach and supervisor. She is director of the MSc in Applied Positive Psychology and Coaching Psychology at the University of East London.

Radical Acceptance

Ingredients

None

When does it work best?

The tool works best when working with clients with high anxiety, resulting from high levels of stress, and when these emotions feel out of control for the client. Like other DBT tools it is best used in combination and as part of a wider DBT approach.

Reference

Lineham, M.M. (1993) *Cognitive Behavioural Treatment for Borderline Personality Disorder*. New York: Guildford Press.

Jonathan Passmore is a chartered psychologist, accredited master coach, team coach, supervisor, author and professor at Henley Business School.

Description

Radical acceptance is an idea drawn from dialectical behavioural therapy (DBT), an approach initially developed to support clients with borderline personality disorder (Lineham, 1993), and has subsequently been used to support clients who experience strong emotional urges and high levels of stress. This technique is focused on looking after yourself in a situation, seeing it for what it really is, without judgement or criticism, and focusing the client's attention on what can be done 'now', as opposed to ruminating about the past and fantasising or imagining possible future consequences and outcomes. The approach, like much of DBT, has similarities with other cognitive behavioural approaches in helping clients identify faulty or unhelpful thinking and redirect their focus to the present moment.

Step by step

1. Invite the client to describe a situation that caused them intense emotions – for example, anxiety, anger or sadness.
2. Explore with the client what the trigger was for this event.
3. Invite the client to explore the physiological sensations in their body that occurred when the event was happening. These may include sweaty palms, raised heart rate, 'boiling blood' or tears.
4. Explore with the client what emotions might sit behind these bodily sensations.
5. The coach should encourage their client not to judge these emotions as 'good' or 'bad', but to accept them for what they are: natural human emotions, felt by everyone and a sign of being human. Nothing more, nothing less.
6. Invite the client to reflect on how they have behaved and what they were thinking about the others in the situation and themselves.
7. Work with the client to develop a proactive plan to move forward that would help them to accept themselves and to accept others, without moving to judge.

Five Ways to Wellbeing

Ingredients

Five Ways to
Wellbeing postcards,
images or your own
postcards or images
to represent the Five
Ways

Paper and pens or
online whiteboard

Description

The Five Ways to Wellbeing is an evidence-based model, intended as a simple
way to help people understand the actions they can take to enhance their own
wellbeing, and the actions that organisations can encourage and support to
promote good mental health in society.

The model was developed by the New Economics Foundation (2008a) for the
Foresight Project's look into mental health, conducted on behalf of the UK
government's Office for Science in 2008. The idea was to produce a
'prescription' for good mental health and wellbeing to mirror the 'five a day'
public health message that encourages people to eat more fruit and vegetables.

The Five Ways are:
- Connect – This is about making and sustaining good relationships with
  friends, family, colleagues and neighbours. NEF says, "Think of these as
  the cornerstones of your life and invest time in developing them. Building
  these connections will support and enrich you every day".
- Be Active – There is much evidence that keeping physically active helps
  promote mental and physical health and reduces illness.
- Take Notice – This is about being curious, noticing the world around you
  and savouring the moment. NEF says, "Be aware of the world around you
  and what you are feeling. Reflecting on your experiences will help you
  appreciate what matters to you".
- Keep Learning – This is about trying something new or rekindling an old
  interest. It is about building confidence as well as doing something fun.
- Give – There is lots of evidence that being useful to others, whether at
  work or home or through volunteering, is key to mental health and
  wellbeing. NEF says, "Seeing yourself, and your happiness, as linked to
  the wider community can be incredibly rewarding and creates connections with the people around you".

Produced as a series of colourful postcards (NEF, 2008b) and spread via an
awareness-raising campaign, the Five Ways model is a useful way to prompt
people into thinking about what is important to them and how they can give
more priority to wellbeing in their daily lives and routines.

Step by step

1. Introduce the model through the postcards. This can be done virtually or
   face-to-face. For visual learners, it can be helpful to use images of fruit
   and vegetables of different colours to represent the Five Ways.

When does it work best?

The model is useful in coaching for resilience, wellbeing, stress management and work–life balance for individuals and teams. While there are many models of wellbeing that can be used in coaching, this is a particularly good framework to use with people working in and around health, social care and the voluntary and community sector in the UK, where it's already well known. People tend to like the NEF graphics and postcards as they are accessible and are written in plain English. They are available as a downloadable resource.

2. You now have a choice:
    a. Use the **GROW model** process to explore the client's current **R**eality in terms of each aspect of wellbeing, their **O**ptions for how to build more of each wellbeing aspect into their day-to-day life, and then **W**rap-up by asking them what actions they **W**ill take to move forward. You can keep it relatively simple by asking person-centred questions like "What's working and not working for you?" for each aspect and "What needs to happen next?"
    b. Use a **Motivational Interviewing** approach by getting the client to score how far they are prioritising each 'Way' on a scale of 1–10 in a graph or pie chart. Ask them why they chose that number and why they didn't choose a higher or lower number. Ask them to identify where they would like to be.
        Help them build confidence in making change through questions like: "Tell me about a time you made changes in your life. How did you do it?"; "What strengths or skills do you have that would help you succeed?"; "Imagine you've made this change already. Looking back, what helped you to make it happen?" and "Who could support you in making this change?"
        Invite them to gauge their commitment and confidence to change by scoring it at the end. Ask how they would overcome any barriers to change and how they will hold themselves to account.
    c. For some clients, a visual/artistic approach can be helpful to explore reality and to surface any conscious and unconscious barriers they might have in prioritising wellbeing in their life. I sometimes get a big piece of paper, divide it into five, then ask the client to draw something in response to how each 'Way' is showing up in their life at the moment and how they feel about it. The client can then be invited to draw something else to represent a future state or something that could inspire or heighten their commitment to achieving an espoused future state or goal.

The beauty of the model is its simplicity; and because there is a wealth of freely available relevant material online, it has been adopted by many organisations across the UK. Have a search for more ideas and have fun!

References

New Economics Foundation (2008a) *Five Ways to Well-being: The Evidence*. Available from: https://neweconomics.org/uploads/files/five-ways-to-wellbeing-1.pdf [Retrieved 23 April 2023].

New Economics Foundation (2008b) 5 Ways Postcards. Available from: https://neweconomics.org/uploads/files/NEF-5ways.pdf [Retrieved 23 April 2023].

Catherine Wilton is a coach, supervisor and leadership development specialist with over 20 years' experience of supporting individuals and groups. She is director of the NHS Leadership for Personalised Care programme and the Collaborative Leadership Academy.

See What We Mean (Team)

Ingredients

A3 paper, flipchart or whiteboard

Coloured pens

Description

Often clients will use an interesting metaphor, simile or analogy for something during a meeting or workshop, when trying to describe an obstacle, goal, issue or circumstance, using a word or phrase to suggest a likeness or analogy. There are already techniques in this book that suggest how exploring metaphors with a client can be useful to create new understanding and pathways. I See What You Mean is useful for working with teams to ask them to reflect together on metaphors used during group or team discussions, and then draw, in large scale, the metaphor they used. As a result, it often creates even richer conversation and comprehension of the situation. The metaphor picture they create provides a way of communicating otherwise-complex information. Drawing it, engaging others in the drawing and making the scale of the drawing large pulls out further details of what is under the surface of the use of the metaphor and facilitates engagement and perspectives from across the group.

When does it work best?

In a team or group setting, this technique creates and supports an opportunity for multiple people to share potentially different views about the same situation, creating clarity and consensus around the issue or objective being discussed.

It can be used at any stage to understand and increase awareness about the situation as it stands today and the team's perception of it. It can be used for unpicking problems, minimising conflict and improving relationships. It can also be used when no metaphor has been offered already and the facilitator challenges the group with a question around the topic, asking the group to generate a metaphor for the situation together, and then to create a drawing from that.

It is best to use this technique when there is no pressure on the time available, its beauty being the ability to pictorially extend the metaphor together, to look at the whole system in which the metaphor or issue described operates. That said, it can also be cut down for use as a quick tension breaker in a group setting, if required.

Step by step

1. Replay the metaphor used by a team or team member to the group.
2. Using a large piece of paper or a whiteboard, ask the person who used the metaphor to draw what they just described when they used this metaphor. Explain the reasons why.
3. The large piece of paper is used to encourage the clients to create an overview and then create or co-create further detail as it is explored further. Allow plenty of time for this and explain that there is no rush.
4. Check that the picture represents what they intended to draw and then use the image to discuss what it represents and the various options and possibilities related to it. A good way to start the more detailed questioning is to use questions like "I'm wondering what/why/how…?" and "Explain a little more about this element of the drawing…?" to engage further thoughts and discussion.
5. Now encourage the client to draw any other aspects of the metaphor outside the system they've already explained through the drawing.
6. Later in the session, or in subsequent sessions, it can be worth referring to this image and the metaphor to develop it further and to demonstrate any changes or idea development by asking how it now fits with their view (or their current reality, if in subsequent session). This will help to reinforce progress made.

Maggie Grieve is an accredited leadership and team development coach, consultant and facilitator with 30 years of working with organisations and leaders across the world. She owns her own business, Ping Thinking, and is an external coach for NHS England.

Gibbs' Reflective Cycle

Ingredients

Pen and paper

Description

Gibbs' Reflective Cycle is a structured approach for reflective practice. It is a practical and easy-to-use implementation of Kolb's learning cycle and Schön's reflection-on-action, which are more conceptual ways of thinking about and analysing personal and professional experiences in order to learn from them. The framework was developed in the 1980s by Graham Gibbs, an educational psychologist. The model can be used during coaching sessions to help clients reflect and learn from experiences. It gives clients a structure to reflect and learn in between coaching sessions, but coaches can also use it on themselves to reflect about and learn from their coaching experiences.

The model consists of six stages:

Description: This is where you describe the situation or experience you are reflecting on. This can include what happened, where it happened, who was involved and any other details you deem relevant.

Feelings: In this stage, you reflect on your feelings about the situation. This could include emotions such as happiness, sadness, anger or confusion. It is important to be honest about your emotions, even if they are uncomfortable.

Evaluation: Here, you evaluate the experience in terms of its positive and negative aspects. You might reflect on what went well and what didn't, what you learned and what you would do differently in the future.

Analysis: This stage involves a deeper analysis of the situation through breaking down the experience. You might consider the underlying causes of the experience, what assumptions you made, and how your actions or the actions of others contributed to the outcome.

Conclusion: In this stage, you draw conclusions about the experience and what you have learned. This might involve identifying areas where you need to improve or recognising strengths and successes.

Action plan: The final stage involves creating an action plan for the future. This might include setting goals, planning how to implement what you have learned, and considering how you will approach similar situations in the future.

Overall, the Gibbs' Reflective Cycle is a useful framework for reflecting on experiences so you or your client can learn from them.

Gibbs' Reflective Cycle

When does it work best?

Gibbs' Reflective Cycle can be used in a variety of contexts and situations, but it is particularly effective in situations where the goal is to learn from experience and improve performance as a coach or as a client. The tool can be used with clients in between coaching sessions, as the tool provides an ideal structure to use when journaling. Using a structure to reflect upon experiences can prevent journaling becoming a written form of rumination.

In general, Gibbs' Reflective Cycle is most effective when used in combination with other tools and approaches, such as feedback and goal setting. It is also important to approach reflection with an open and curious mindset, and to be willing to learn from both positive and negative experiences.

Step by step

Gibbs' Reflective Cycle works through answering questions step by step, either in a conversation or written in a journal:

1. **Description**: What happened?
2. **Feelings**: What were you thinking and feeling?
3. **Evaluation**: What was good and what was bad?
4. **Analysis**: What sense can you make of the situation?
5. **Conclusion**: What else could you have done?
6. **Action plan**: If it occurs again, what would you do?

Reference

Gibbs, G. (1988) *Learning by Doing: A Guide to Teaching and Learning Methods*. Further Education Unit.

Marc Innegraeve is an accredited executive and team coach and a researcher. He holds an MSc in coaching and behavioural change from Henley.

Nine Questions

Ingredients

Diagram

Flipchart or digital whiteboard

Description

One challenge often faced by teams is a lack of a shared agreement as to their purpose, and the respective roles and rules for the team. The Nine Questions tool is a simple way for the team to explore these aspects and through a conversation create a shared understanding. Using a team coach, who can challenge and encourage the team members to move beyond superficial answers, means areas of potential future conflict or confusion can be unearthed and resolved.

Where do we operate? (Focus)	Why are we here? (Purpose)	Who are our allies? (Supporters)
Who does what? (Roles)	What guides us? (Values)	How do we work together? (Team contract)
How should we work when things go wrong? (Crisis)	What do we need to learn?	What do we need to focus on now? (Priorities)

When does it work best?

This tool is a good starting place for a new team that is establishing the what, why and how of working together, or a team with new members.

Step by step

1. The team coach shares the diagram and explains the process.
2. The team coach works with the team to explore each question. The order should be decided by the team.
3. As with most creative exercises, time should be provided for some individual reflection and note taking, before the ideas are shared and then discussed to craft a shared answer for each question.
4. The team coach facilitates the process, probing, challenging and encouraging deeper exploration, while the team owns the output, which it should capture on a digital whiteboard or flipchart.

Jonathan Passmore is a chartered psychologist, accredited ICF executive coach, coach supervisor, author and professor at Henley Business School.

Flight Tracker

Ingredients

1 Crib sheet (until it's second nature)

Description

Flight Tracker is a technique that prompts the coach to address key areas at the start of a coaching session, during the main body of the session and as the session draws to a close.

The terms **TAKE OFF**, **IN FLIGHT** and **LANDING** are used as acronyms derived from the first letter of each of these key components, each representing a word that guides the coach through important areas to cover in the opening, middle and end segments of the session. The author has been using versions of this in her coaching for many years and has 'tested' it with other coaches by introducing it into supervision conversations.

Some examples of questions are offered here: these are simply for starters; find your own words and ask them in your own way.

When does it work best?

This is an effective framework for any coaching conversation. It is especially useful for addressing the coach's responsibility to honour and manage the 'task' of the session in the time available to complete it. It prompts the coach to contract clearly for the session timeframe, and guides the client towards identifying and articulating a clear, simply stated outcome of their choosing to be addressed in that time. This helps to set the destination and the direction of travel for both the coach and the client in common language that both can refer to as the session evolves.

There are times when a client arrives with a grand-scale topic on their minds, with a full head or not quite able to put their finger on what they want. Sometimes the coach may themselves feel distracted, be overwhelmed by the client's content or be tempted to lead the conversation.

This framework can be helpful to ensure the session addresses a range of dimensions, priorities and perspectives, and that the client is encouraged to engage with fresh thinking and to draw upon their learning and its application in real time.

These three acronyms – **TAKE OFF**, **IN FLIGHT** and **LANDING** – introduce a light-touch structural discipline, supportive of the coach, the client and the integrity of the session itself.

Flight Tracker

Step by step

1. Explain to the client that you would like to use the three acronyms to help guide the session and make it as effective as possible.
2. You may wish to sketch these out with the client or just describe them verbally.
3. Use the questions or expand on these by using your own to help tease out the coaching conversation.
4. Summarise and evaluate the usefulness of the session and any takeaways as you normally would with the client.

TOPIC	What would you like to talk about?
	What's on your mind?
ATTENTION	What's calling for your attention?
	How is this affecting you?
KERNEL	What's at the heart of this?
	What do you want to focus on?
END	By the end of this session…
OBJECTIVE	…where would you like to get to?
FEW WORDS	How can you capture that in a few words?
FIRST	What do you want to talk about first?
	Where do you want to start?

IMPORTANT	What makes this important for you?
	What matters to you here?
NOW	What's the situation now?
	How is this playing out at the moment?
FUTURE	How will things be different when you've addressed this?
	What's your hope for the future?
LEVERAGE	What can you influence?
	Where can you make some changes?

Flight Tracker

INSIGHTS	What are you becoming aware of? What ideas are popping up?
GUT	What's your gut telling you? How does that feel?
HEAD	What do you think? What information do you need?
TIMECHECK	In the time we have left [state the remaining time], what needs to happen? How does that 'sit' with your objective for this session?

LEARNING	What are you learning about the situation? What are you learning about yourself?
ACTION	What's your way forward? What could you do to make progress?
NEEDS	How can you get support for that? Who/what do you need around you?
DERAIL	What could knock you off track? What challenges can you foresee?
INTENTIONS	How will you tackle these? What's your plan?
NEXT	What happens next? How will you begin?
GO!	How shall we end today's session? Ready to go?

Ann James is an accredited coach, supervisor, author and trainer of coaches.

Shared Reminiscence

Ingredients

None

Description

"Do you remember when we…?" This exercise uses a simple storytelling structure to help people connect and develop a sense of shared history and success. Derived from improvised theatre, shared reminiscence about an imaginary event in the past helps to foster connection and collaboration, as well as building listening skills, creativity and resourcefulness. It can then be repeated with a focus on a real goal, as if the person or team are looking back on a past success.

Step by step

1. When working with a team, ask someone to suggest an idea for an imaginary success they have achieved together in the past, for example: "when we won *Britain's Got Talent*".
2. The team will then tell the story, one sentence and one person at a time, of how they got there. Ask the team to arrange themselves in an order (e.g. a circle or numbered on a virtual screen).
3. One person will start with "Do you remember the time we…?" and invent the starting point for the story.
4. The next person will then respond with "Yes, and…", each time building on the last thing that was said, to build and progress the story.
5. Carry on for a number of rounds, or until the team reaches the point at which they achieved their imaginary success.
6. Celebrate the achievement!
7. As a coach, you may need to step in to encourage shifts in energy, support clients to avoid 'over-thinking' and to push for a conclusion (e.g. one more round).
8. In the debrief, help the team to reflect on the "What?", "So what?" and "Now what?" for how they work together and what this means for how they feel about and will seek to progress towards their own shared endeavour.
9. It may then be helpful to repeat the same exercise using a real goal. Themes such as motivation, resourcefulness and dealing with setbacks are likely to surface.
10. To adapt this exercise for an individual, ask them to progress the story themselves, but perhaps taking a little more time to really listen and react to what they have just said. As a coach, you can also provide useful feedback in terms of what you noticed with respect to body language and patterns of behaviour.

Julie Flower is a leadership development coach, consultant and facilitator, with a specialism in improvisation in complex systems. She is also an external tutor in executive coaching at Henley Business School.

Killing the Ravana

Description

According to the *Ramayana* (Hinduism's holy scripture), Lord Rama, the goddess Sita (Rama's wife) and his brother Laxman were exiled in forests for fourteen years. While in the forests, Sita was abducted by Ravana, the demon king of Lanka. He imprisoned Sita in Lanka.

Accompanied by his brother Laxman and an army of monkeys, Lord Rama went to Lanka to battle Ravana so that he could free Sita from captivity. Lord Rama and his allies started a fierce battle with Ravana and his allies. In the last days of the battle, Lord Rama was exhausted, worried and felt sad. At that time, Sage Agastya came to Lord Rama and advised him to pray to the sun god by chanting a holy mantra thrice. He told Lord Rama that by doing this he would get the victory by killing Ravana. Sage Agastya told Lord Rama the various benefits of chanting that holy mantra.

After listening to Sage Agastya's advice, Lord Rama's sadness disappeared. Lord Rama with a happy heart completed the prayers and rituals as per the advice of Sage Agastya. Lord Rama was very pleased after completing the rituals. After that he took his bow and looked at Ravana and enthusiastically proceeded to conquer. He determined to kill Ravana with all his efforts.

When Lord Rama was moving towards Ravana to kill him, the sun god appeared and told Lord Rama that the time of Ravana's death was near and he advised Lord Rama to kill him immediately. Lord Rama followed his advice and killed Ravana.

When does it work best?

This tool works best when the coach feels that the client is feeling tired and sad because of not achieving success in spite of their efforts. Sometimes the client has lost hope and enthusiasm due to a lack of accomplishments. This is well suited when the coach observes, through the client's narrative, that the client is not hopeful and there is a need to help the client get enthusiastic about their goals and efforts.

Step by step

1. Ask the client if they have heard of the *Ramayana*, Lord Rama, Sita and Ravana.
2. Share with them briefly this episode from the *Ramayana*.
3. Invite the client to share their previous activities or rituals that might have helped in enhancing positive mental states such as joy and happiness. The activities may be from any sphere or stage of life. The client may also think of activities done by their parents or grandparents, or if they have a faith, something that is part of their faith practice.
4. The coach invites the client to elaborate on these activities and how they enhanced positive emotions in them.
5. The coach may also invite the client to think of activities and rituals which might have filled them with hope and enthusiasm in the past. They may also enquire about the activities/actions which can help the client in enhancing their hope and enthusiasm in the current context.

Killing the Ravana

6. By connecting with the determination of Lord Rama to kill Ravana, the coach may also ask questions around what may enhance the determination of the client to achieve their goals. The coach may also ask questions about what may help the client in exerting all out efforts to achieve their goals.
7. Lord Rama's wife was in the prison of Ravana, so he had a strong reason (a motivation or 'big why') to fight with Ravana and kill him. The coach also enquires about their client's reasons for wanting to accomplish that particular goal.
8. The coach invites the client to visualise some of the activities or rituals in their mind's eye.
9. After the visualisation, the coach enquires of the client about their new level of enthusiasm and determination towards the achievement of their goal.
10. The coach also invites the client to formulate learning from the inputs generated in the previous steps.
11. The coach enquires of the client about how they will use this new learning for the accomplishment of their goals.

Dr Badri Bajaj is a leading coach and researcher, and imparts coaching training to individuals and organisations.

APB Model of Humankind

Ingredients

Image of the model

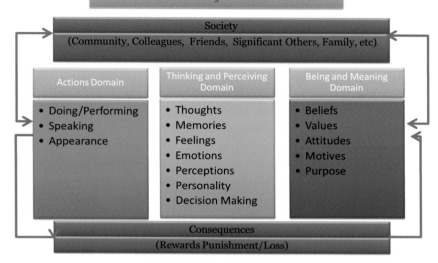

When does it work best?

The APB model can be most useful to enable clients to explore the whole human being in a holistic manner, without being stuck in a particular philosophy or school of thought. By considering all three domains, plus the system (society) and the impact of their actions, thinking or being, a fuller understanding can be achieved.

Note: The diagram is used with permission of Mongezi Makhalima.

Mongezi C. Makhalima is an OD specialist, TEDx speaker and chartered coach with 30 years of working with organisations and leaders across the world.

Description

This came up when a young client of mine asked me "Why are people so complicated?" and I proceeded to describe 150 years of psychology in 30 minutes. This description eventually synthesised into this model.

The APB model is perhaps an expanded Iceberg model, lying on its side, that helps both the coach and the client to navigate different levels of their psychological attributes to figure out which areas impact coaching outcomes the most. It can be a source of powerful questions about the content of the client's state of being beyond process questions.

Step by step

1. Share the model with the client, describing each of the three domains, and the streams of society/stakeholders and consequences and rewards.
2. Invite the client to consider which domains might be impacting on the issue they are presenting.
3. Explore this domain with the client.
4. Invite the client to consider whether other domains may be having an impact, and explore this.
5. Continue the process, until the client believes they have exhausted all domains, and have insights or actions from each to help them to move forward.

Developing Self-compassion through Chair Work

Ingredients

Empty chair

When does it work best?

The technique can be used to help clients with low self-esteem, and works through helping the client first to connect with compassion for others they care for and then to apply this to themselves.

Description

This technique is drawn from cognitive behavioural coaching and its fusion with techniques from Gestalt chair work. The technique invites the client to imagine the personal sensation of compassion, and to project this compassion towards someone who they care about and who is experiencing the same feelings as the client, but who is occupying the empty chair. By exploring the other's experience and rational thoughts in the situation, the client can gain new insight about themselves and how a more self-compassionate perspective may help.

Step by step

1. The coach identifies an issue with low self-esteem held by the client. This may be expressed by the client as anxiety, guilt or shame.
2. The coach invites the client to close their eyes and to notice their breathing.
3. The coach next invites the client to imagine their body filling up with a refreshing liquid of compassion, which slowly rises from the toes to the top of their head, filling them top to toe with loving compassion.
4. The coach introduces an empty chair and invites the client to bring to mind a person who the client cares about, such as a close friend or family member.
5. The coach invites the client to imagine this named person experiencing the same feelings as a result of a similar situation – for example, feeling worried about a job interview.
6. The coach invites the client to consider how that person might be feeling, and then whether such feelings are helpful. Usually, the client feels a sense of compassion towards the other individual, and believes that the feelings the other individual has are not helpful, logical or evidence-based.
7. The coach invites the client to express in words their compassion towards the empty chair and the person they imagine to be sitting there.
8. Once the client has finished speaking, the coach invites the client to reflect on the experience. What have they learnt about their own situation? How can they apply this compassionate side of themselves to the situation they themselves face?
9. The coach and client continue to explore this together in more depth.

Jonathan Passmore is a chartered psychologist, accredited master executive coach, team coach, supervisor, author and professor at Henley Business School.

*Developing Self-
compassion
through Chair
Work*

Dancefloor to the Balcony

Ingredients

None

Description

Schön's reflection-in-action is a concept in the field of education and professional practice that describes a type of reflective practice that occurs in the moment, during the process of doing something (Schön, 1968). It is a form of reflection that involves reflecting on and adjusting one's actions and decision-making in real-time, as the situation unfolds.

According to Schön, professionals engage in reflection-in-action when they are faced with a situation that is unfamiliar or ambiguous, and they must make decisions quickly and adapt to changing circumstances. In these situations, professionals rely on their intuition and previous experience to make judgements, but they also reflect on their actions and adjust their approach as needed.

To achieve this reflection-in-action, Ronald Heifetz introduced the concept "from the dancefloor to the balcony" (Heifetz and Linsky, 2002). This "from the dancefloor to the balcony" metaphor is used to describe the importance of stepping back from a situation and gaining perspective to see the bigger picture and identify potential solutions, as well as to increase insight into your own behaviour. It is based on the idea that, when you're on the dancefloor, where the action is with its friction, noise and tension, you're focused on the immediate experience and can't see the larger patterns at play. However, when you move to the balcony, you can see the whole dancefloor and how the different parts fit together, including the behaviour of different persons – yourself and others – that shape the interaction. Once on the balcony, several coaching approaches are possible, depending on the needs of the client.

According to Heifetz, leaders need to be able to switch easily between the 'dancefloor' and the 'balcony'. The dancefloor represents the action and energy of the moment, while the balcony represents a higher perspective and a more detached view of the situation. By switching between these perspectives, leaders can better understand the dynamics at play and make more informed decisions.

Role Reversal

Ingredients

Private room with some space

Callum O'Neill is a BPS registered psychologist and ICF accredited coach (PCC).

When does it work best

Role Reversal is particularly effective when clients are struggling to understand the perspectives of others or when there are communication breakdowns or conflicts in relationships. It can be used to help clients build empathy and emotional intelligence, particularly in leadership development programs, team coaching, and diversity and inclusion training. It may also be useful for exploring abstract concepts such as fear, anger or self-doubt.

Description

Role Reversal is a coaching intervention that helps clients see a situation from a different perspective by stepping into the shoes of another person or concept. It is derived from psychodrama, a therapeutic approach developed by Jacob Levy Moreno that emphasises the use of drama, action methods and role playing to help individuals gain a deeper understanding of their emotions and behaviours by exploring different perspectives of their issues in a safe and supportive environment. Role Reversal is designed to help clients develop empathy, emotional intelligence and a more nuanced understanding of their relationships with others. By stepping into another person's shoes, clients can gain new insights into their own behaviour and motivations, as well as those of others. This can help them to identify and address interpersonal issues, improve communication and collaboration, and develop a more rounded perspective on their personal and professional lives.

Step by step

1. Begin by identifying a specific interpersonal situation or concept that the client would like to work on. The client should choose someone or something they want to better understand.
2. Invite the client to identify the person involved in the situation and to describe the situation from their own perspective.
3. Next, the client should physically move to a new position in the room and assume the physical stance and gestures of the other person or concept. Ask the client to imagine themselves in the other person's shoes, and to describe the situation from that person's perspective. This can be done through guided visualisation, journaling or by simply asking the client to imagine themselves in the other person's position. The client may find it useful to assume the physical stance and gestures of the other person or concept.
4. Encourage the client to explore the situation from the other person's perspective, focusing on their motivations, feelings and behaviours.
5. After the client has spent some time imagining themselves in the other person's shoes, ask them to switch back to their own perspective and reflect on what they have learned from the exercise.
6. Use open-ended questions to encourage the client to explore any new insights or understanding they have gained from the exercise.
7. Develop a plan of action to help the client address any interpersonal issues or conflicts that may have been identified during the exercise.

References

Blatner, A. (2000) *Foundations of Psychodrama: History, Theory, and Practice* (4th edition). Berlin: Springer Publishing.

Kipper, D.A. (2002) The Cognitive Double: Integrating Cognitive and Action Techniques. *Journal of Group Psychotherapy: Psychodrama & Sociometry*, 55: 93–106.

Moreno, J.L. (1985) *Psychodrama*. Beacon, NY: Beacon House.

Unsticking with Pictures

Ingredients

A children's illustrated dictionary

Description

It's not uncommon for clients to encounter a feeling of being stuck. This can manifest in them struggling to formulate solutions or having difficulty making forward progress on goals. Sometimes it can be helpful to use some unexpected and external resources to help facilitate the breakthroughs your clients need to enable them to move forward on their journey to goal attainment.

This tool follows the approach of seeking other influences, in this case a child's picture dictionary, to help a client find a new way of approaching a problem when they are 'stuck'; in this respect, it is similar to tools involving the selection of random objects or words. In this case, the client is encouraged to look for pictures and words that resonate with the topic they wish to explore and then to use the thoughts that these images provoke to work with the coach to expand on their issue or challenge.

Step by step

1. Give the client the picture dictionary. Ask them to look through it and pick a page at random. The client should then be asked to select the word they find most interesting or relevant.
2. Ask the client to talk about their situation for about five minutes, using the word selected in the previous step.
3. Together, coach and client should carry on developing and expanding their conversation using the new insights gained from Step 2.

Reference

Van Niewerburgh, C. (2014) *An Introduction to Coaching Skills: A Practical Guide*. London: Sage.

Maggie Grieve is an accredited leadership and team development coach, consultant and facilitator with 30 years of working with organisations and leaders across the world. She owns her own business, Ping Thinking, and is an external coach for NHS England.

Disagree and Commit

Ingredients

Attitude: open-mindedness and a willingness to commit

Note taking

Description

Teams disagree for several reasons including status and power, the need for control, wanting to be right, saving face and so on. The unintended consequences of this can lead to cliques, scapegoating and apathy.

We also know that when group efforts are not aligned towards a common cause, goal or task, collective energy becomes dispersed, hampering progress. In the most challenging environments, a team may be caught in a cycle of disagreement, abstention and artificial harmony.

Disagree and Commit has been adapted from the work of Patrick Lencioni (2005), whose leadership model sets out five limiting characteristics (dysfunctions) that teams can fall into. These are outlined in the pyramid below. The method offers groups and teams an effective way to improve decision-making and manage conflict.

Inattention to **Results** — Focus on delivering measurable results

Avoidance of **Accountability** — To take accountability requires prior commitment

Lack of **Commitment** — Commitment follows healthy conflict

Fear of **Conflict** — Healthy conflict implies candid debate

Absence of **Trust** — Building trust requires vulnerability

When does it work best?

This tool works best when there is no obvious right or wrong answer for the team's decision and when opinion is split on how to move forward. With practice, this process builds democracy, deepens listening skills and encourages leaders to respect the views of others without unhelpful interruptions. It is also a useful tool to defuse tension and manage contributions from more difficult colleagues.

Step by step

Buy in

1. Begin by acknowledging any unrest and the topic of contention.
2. Describe the Disagree and Commit principle to settle people and to advise that the disagreement will be resolved democratically by the end of the process.
3. Invite the team/group lead to collate views so that all contributions have been noted.
4. Advise the group that each member will have a minute or two to have their say, including the team/group lead.
5. Now, taking turns, invite each member to put their thoughts, views and ideas forward. It is very important during this step to hear everyone out and manage any interruptions.
6. Following the final contribution, invite the team/group lead to summarise the discussion and the options arising from this process and allow two-to-three minutes to do this.

Voting

7. Invite each member of the group to vote for their preferred option, including the team/group lead. The majority view will determine the outcome of the decision, even if the leader's vote was part of a minority view. If the group has an even number and the decision is split equally, the group shall then defer to the team leader to make the final decision, irrespective of how each member voted.

Clarify and commit

8. Summarise what has been agreed and seek confirmation that each member is willing either to agree or to disagree *and* commit to the decision. The principle behind this step is that the decision now belongs *to the group* and not merely to any one member within it, including the leader. Decision-making in this way will help foster openness, build trust and improve team cohesion.

Reference

Lencioni, P. (2005) *Overcoming the Five Dysfunctions of a Team*.

Note: Diagram used with the permission of Karen Hayns.

Karen Hayns is a Henley-trained business, lifestyle and health coach with a corporate background spanning three decades.

Lego Coaching: Exploring the Gap

Ingredients

Lego (any amount or type)

Description

Exploring the gap with Lego Coaching (i.e. coaching with small bricks) allows clients the space and time to build a new awareness of their current situation and what their desired outcome would look like. Using the Triple-E method of Lego Coaching – Engage, Explore and Expand (Quinn and Bab, 2021) – clients are encouraged to engage with both the Lego and the build question, to explore with model building and to expand their thoughts on what they would like to have happen to move closer to their desired outcome.

The client initially builds a model that represents their current state. Next, they are invited to build a model that represents their desired outcome. With the two models side by side, the client is then invited to explore the gap between them. This can be through coaching questions and/or building further models.

Slowing the coaching process down allows for greater reflection, creation of new awareness and using new learning to create positive growth or change.

Step by step

Prior to the session, ensure that you are familiar with using Lego and have tried the build question yourself.

1. Frame the building opportunity with your client to ensure that it is a relevant question for them.
2. **Engage** the client with a warm-up build task so that they feel comfortable using Lego.
3. Share the first build task with the client: "Build a model that enables you to answer the question 'What does my current state look like?' You can take up to 20 minutes to complete your build". During this **Explore** stage of the session, allow the client time and space to build silently, whilst being there to answer any questions they may have.
4. Share the second build task: "Build a model that enables you to answer the question 'What do I want my desired outcome to look like?' You can take up to 20 minutes to complete your build". Again, allow them to **Explore** as before.
5. Invite the client to place their models side by side with a gap in between them and invite them to share what they have built with you.
6. Use coaching questions to allow the client to explore further – for example, "What's missing?", "What could you add?", "What difference will it make to you to move from model one to model two?" or "What does/could the gap look like?" This is an opportunity for the client to reflect on their models and consider different ideas and perspectives.

Lego Coaching: Exploring the Gap

7. **Expand** these new insights either with new models that are placed in the gap or are used to connect the two models, and/or with further questions, such as "What would need to happen to move from model one to model two?", "What are you already doing that is working that you could do more of?", "What is the next small, actionable step you could take today?" or "How will it look, feel, be when you move closer to your desired outcome?"

Reference

Quinn, T., and Bab, M. (2021) LEGO® SERIOUS PLAY® in 1–1 Coaching. In W.A. Smith, I. Boniwell and S. Green (eds), *Positive Psychology Coaching in the Workplace*. Springer, Cham.

Theresa Quinn is a coaching psychologist and PhD researcher, exploring the experience of coaching with small bricks for both neurodiverse and neurotypical clients.

Personal Board of Directors

Ingredients

None

When does it work best?

The technique can be used with almost all clients during the early stages of coaching to help clients to recognise they are not working alone and that, by drawing together a support team, their chances of making real progress will be enhanced.

Description

One element that many clients neglect is how they can leverage their personal network of clients, family and colleagues to help them achieve their goals. This technique seeks to address the challenge that, while the coach may meet the client once a week or once a month, between meetings the client needs to call upon their own resources to make progress. For every hour in a coaching conversation, there are a further 100 hours (or more) of time when the client has to find their own way forward.

The personal board of directors is a metaphor to which many clients can relate. One way this can be introduced, depending on the individual's cultural background and age, is by referring to the popular 1980s American TV show *The A Team* and inviting the client to consider who is in their own personal A Team, to support, encourage, resource and hold them to account. This technique helps clients recognise they are not alone, and if they call upon friends, family members and colleagues to support them, providing advice, encouragement, championing them when they slip back, as well as holding them to account, they are more likely to achieve their goal than if they try to achieve behavioural change by themselves.

Step by step

1. Introduce the idea to the client, possibly with a story or an explanation of the metaphor – a personal board of directors.
2. Invite the client to reflect on what they need to help them move forward: resources, someone to encourage them, someone to hold them to account.
3. Invite the client to identify who might undertake each role on their board, and how and when they will invite that person to accept that role.

Jonathan Passmore is a chartered psychologist, accredited master coach, team coach, supervisor, author and professor at Henley Business School.

Four Energy Cylinders Check

Ingredients

Paper or flipchart

Pens or markers

Description

To be at our best, we need energy. We spend energy in doing and need to replenish it. But different activities come with different energetic requirements. For example, we need a great deal of physical energy to complete a fitness task and much more cognitive energy to get through the company's annual report.

Today's busy lives, with most people having multiple roles and responsibilities with ever less time to rest and recharge, place ever greater demands on our current energy levels. This means it can be easy to overexert, be habitually depleted and eventually burn out. Four Energy Cylinders is a simple and effective tool to assess what energy we have available, track whether we're recovering or draining, and discover best practices that help us replenish.

To achieve this, we begin by dividing energy into four intuitive sources or 'energy cylinders':
- Physical (P) – the energy our bodies hold to run a mile, for example
- Mental (M) – the energy our brains have to solve problems
- Spiritual (S) – the energy of our essence, spirit or will
- Emotional (E) – the energy available in our heart.

While some tasks demand one main energy cylinder, many require a specific combination. If a given cylinder runs down, we can draw on the others in the short term, but if we don't routinely top up our overall wellbeing, our productivity levels, results and relationships will suffer. Persistently low cylinders present serious risks of chronic fatigue, isolation, depression and burnout.

Four Energy Cylinders is a simple and effective tool to develop energy-level awareness for vital self-care and healthy sustainable performance. It can also be used to support burnout recovery. Four Energy Cylinders offers an intuitive and useful framework to develop awareness about our internal resources, how we spend them and how we can replenish them. It can be used as a daily self-care practice, in wellbeing coaching and burnout recovery, as well as to support healthy personal leadership.

Step by step

1. **Introducing the Four Energy Cylinders concept:** In this step we can draw a simple schematic as above or use the four letters P, M, S, E to designate the four different energy sources.
2. **Assessing energy levels with calibration**
   At your best
   We invite clients to bring to mind a situation or moment when they felt at their best. As our personal best is always changing, this helps clients find their most appropriate personal benchmark and avoid external, and often unhelpful, comparisons.

Four Energy Cylinders Check

We may say, "Could you take a moment and bring to your awareness a time when you achieved something that felt energising and left you feeling at your best? Something you completed in 'full flow'. It could be a dinner you prepared, a presentation you gave or how you can recall yourself getting out of bed in the morning."

"I wonder if you can tell me about the state of your four energy levels in this scenario?"

"Perhaps you can express them as a percentage or in some other manner that has meaning for you."

"How would you describe and/or rate your physical energy level? Mental energy level? Spiritual energy level? Emotional energy level?"

"How does it feel to remember them now?"

Today or the present moment

Then, we invite clients to explore what is true for them now. We may say, "Coming back to the present moment, I wonder if you can tell me how your energy levels are right now?"

Again, make reference to the energy cylinder for Body (physical), Mind, Spirit and Heart.

3. **Helping clients resource effectively**: We invite the client to consider something they want to achieve or complete and we may even ask them to place this in one of their hands as if to weigh it up against the energy that is available. We may say, "Given the task you want to achieve and your current energy cylinders as they are, are you up to the task?"
   If the answer is yes, the client will receive a natural boost of motivation as they and you, as coach, can affirm there is no impediment to action and focus them on the value of the process and outcome.
   If the answer is no, we can coach the client to identify additional resources they need. We may say, "Notice what seems to be missing. Any ideas on how you could address this, either within yourself or by getting additional help?"

4. **Exploring what feeling topped up will look and feel like**: We invite the client into a future where their physical, mental, spiritual and emotional cylinders are fully recharged and explore what this might be like and how it came to be this way.

5. **Setting goals**: We convert possibility into a goal or positive direction the client can use.

6. **Exploring options**: We work with the client to come up with ideas they have tried, things they may want to try and also ideas they would perhaps not dare to try, as a way to generate a healthy pool of choices to choose from.

7. **Commitment and accountability**: Here we invite the client to decide what they will do and how they will gauge progress. They may choose to use the energy cylinders for themselves or find another way.

8. **Closing the work and wishing them well**: We may close the work by inviting the client to affirm something about their energy cylinders. For example:
   - "I look forward to topping up my spiritual cylinder."
   - "Having a healthy level of physical energy is important to me."

References

Bak-Maier, M. (2019) *Body Talk: How to Tap into Your Super Power for Health and Wellbeing.* Make Time Count Ltd.

Bak-Maier, M. (2015) *Get Productive Grid.* Make Time Count Ltd.

Bak-Maier, M. (2012) *Get Productive! Boosting Your Productivity and Getting Things Done.* Capstone.

Dr Magdalena Bak-Maier is an international teacher and coach trainer who helps people reconnect with their full potential.

Wellbeing at Work Model

Ingredients

Picture or drawing of the Wellbeing at Work Model (Figure 1)

Pen(s)

Paper

Whiteboard or flipchart

When does it work best?

This model works best when a client wants to explore and grow awareness of their own wellbeing in their work context. It is particularly useful for clients who work as helping professionals. It can be used as a proactive tool for when people's wellbeing is good, to understand what is working and how this state of wellbeing can be maintained. It can also be used to explore strategies to improve people's wellbeing at work.

Description

A person's individual wellbeing and self-management of wellbeing form complex and widely interpreted topics. The Wellbeing at Work Model (McEwen and Rowson, 2022) is a conceptual model that can be used with clients (and coaches themselves in self-reflection and/or supervision) to deepen their understanding of their own wellbeing at work. The model demonstrates the dynamics that sit with three interrelated themes that can influence people's wellbeing at work.

Levels of wellbeing: Wellbeing levels can change and fluctuate while people are at work. There will be individual cues that people will experience when their wellbeing is high and when wellbeing levels are lower. It is useful for people to understand their own unique cues for changes in wellbeing and then how to respond to/recognise these early.

Self-regulation: How people maintain and manage their wellbeing can be linked to the active self-management on a day-to-day basis. The use of self-regulation practices helps optimise people's resources and energy. It may include managing workloads or capacity, scheduling, learning to say yes when you need to and no when you need to, or job crafting (see Job Crafting tool). Using self-regulation proactively and regularly can help people's wellbeing at work.

Energy currents: Depending upon the nature of work or specific job demands, there can be ebbs and flows of energy at work. There may be times when work can be 'quite tiring' and times when it is 'energising'. It is sometimes also difficult to notice changes in energy and therefore important for people to understand their own energy currents when they work.

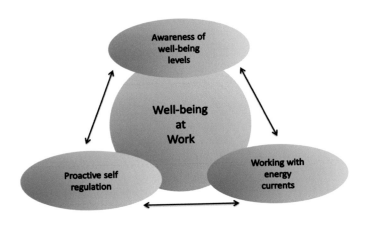

Figure 1. The dynamics of individual well-being at work.

Step by step

1. Explain the model to the client in the coaching session.
2. Invite the client to find three objects in the room that represent energy currents, levels of wellbeing or self-regulation, or to use the picture or drawing of the model.
3. Discuss each of these objects (or theme/area of the model) in depth – for example, by asking "what drew you to this object for this theme/area?", "What does this mean here and now for you at work?", "What physical, psychological or behavioural cues would you experience if this theme/ area was going well for you?", "What cues would you experience if things were not going so well for you?" or "What gets your attention most?"
4. Encourage the client to write any insights down.
5. Discuss what changes the client feels they need to make in terms of supporting their wellbeing at work. Encourage them to explore how they will bring these to life at work.
6. The model can also be used as a frame of reference for observing the dynamics of wellbeing. For example, using a daily reflection log over a set period of time in which people self-monitor their energy currents, levels of wellbeing or self-regulation strategies and any individual cues they may experience. This can then be discussed in depth at the next coaching session.

Reference

McEwen, D., and Rowson, T. (2022) 'Saying Yes When You Need to and No When You Need To': An Interpretative Phenomenological Analysis of Coaches' Well-being. *Coaching: An International Journal of Theory, Research and Practice*, 16(1): 59–71.

Deb McEwen is an experienced accredited coach who has held senior leadership roles (NZ, AU and UK) and has an extensive background in health and wellbeing.

The Danger of Using Tools

While this book focuses exclusively on tools, we don't want you to assume tools are the end-all and be-all of coaching. In fact, we believe it's quite the reverse. Coaching is essentially a relationship between two people. In Carl Rogers' language, one, the coach, is congruent within the relationship; the other, the client, brings incongruence, in the form of an issue, a problem or a topic to be explored. Of course, in reality, we are all incongruent. We all have dilemmas, troubles, anxieties or emotions. This congruence–incongruence relationship means that, unlike a 'normal conversation' between friends, which moves back and forward between their respective interests or concerns, in coaching, all the focus is towards the interests or concerns of the client.

This unique feature of coaching means that the coach needs to bring with them a high level of skill in managing the process, thus enabling the client to remain focused on their content. Effective coaches are able to draw on advanced inter-personal skills – listening, summarising, reflecting, affirming, using silence and questions – to help the client navigate their way through the process and emerge with new insights, plans and personal learning. It is these skills that are the basic ingredients of effective coaching. Only once these basic skills have been mastered should the coach turn to tools to assist in the exploration and navigation of the journey.

When offered a 'cookbook of tools', there are a host of dangers lying ahead for the novice coach presented with such an array. We would advocate being mindful of potential pitfalls, which can help the coach stay focused on the core ingredients and keep in mind that tools are but the cherries on the cake.

So, here are five dangers of coaching tools:

1. **The law of the instrument:** One of the biggest dangers is the coach who has a tool and uses it in every situation. Maslow's Hammer, as this dilemma is known, is a common challenge for us all. We may be highly skilled in using a particularly tool, but the question is: is it the right tool for this client, for this issue or at this moment in the conversation? Our view is that by creating a massive toolbox, coaches can expand their repertoire and thus have 50 or 100 tools in their toolkit, not just five or ten.

2. **Coaching tools beat listening:** A second danger is a belief that tools can always get us out of a situation. Instead, we would argue that returning to listening and reflecting back is almost always more powerful than a tool. Tools are an amazing resource, but only when combined with the core coaching skills.

3. **The magic of the tool:** A third danger of tools is the way they are intro-duced. Some coaches might be tempted to suggest to clients that the tool is a form of magic or creates a transformational moment. While new insights can emerge from their use, we would advocate lowering client expectations. One way to do this is by using the word 'experiment':

"Would you be happy to try an experiment? We have found that some clients sometimes find this helpful". This allows the client to find it *not* helpful, and thus for the experiment to fail. Nothing is lost, and the coach and client can continue on their journey.

4. **I have never done it before:** The fourth danger is experimenting with a new tool on paying clients. We would advocate that you find ways to practise the first two or three times with peers (for example, on a course) or when providing pro-bono coaching, but making it clear in your contracting that you will be trying out new tools and approaches you may not have used before. This allows you to develop the 'script' to introduce the tool and get a sense of how it lands with different clients before you start using it with paying clients.

5. **Look how clever I am:** The final danger is that the tool becomes a 'party piece', which the coach believes demonstrates to the client just how wonderful they are. This is most likely to happen when the coach focuses on their signature tools. We would suggest being a Jack or Jill of all trades, capable of using many tools, and using the one that you believe is best for your client and their specific situation.

The Best Coaching Question in the World

Ingredients

An open mind

When does it work best

The first answer someone gives you is almost never the only answer, and it's rarely the best answer. "And what else?" is the quickest and easiest way to uncover and create new possibilities whatever the circumstance.

Description

Most coaches aren't lazy enough. They are working too hard. Coaches are often so keen to be useful and to prove that they're adding value and contributing mightily, that they miss a trick on how *actually* to be helpful. What changes everything is when you realise that the first answer someone gives you to a question is not their only answer and rarely their best answer. It's just their first answer. They're just getting warmed up. Instead, the first answer often works as bait. The coach bites, and everyone gets ensnared on that presenting challenge. People's advice monsters arrive at the party, and suddenly we're all busy trying to solve the wrong problem.

Instead, "And what else?" is the best coaching question in the world. It holds the space of curiosity open longer and finds the most useful place to go. It's different from "Tell me more". This and its variations invite people to expand on the answer that's already been given. "And what else?" is saying, "I'm sure there are other insights/answers/challenges. What are they?" Part of the magic is that, most times, the person you're coaching will not have realised what else is going on. It's not a question that forces them to reveal what they're hiding so much as it helps them discover what they hadn't realised they already knew.

Step by step

1. You ask a question. They answer.
2. You say something encouraging about the answer – "That's great" – and ask, "And what else?"
3. They answer again. There's almost always something else to say.
4. You nod, look enthusiastic and curious, and ask again, "And what else?"
5. You repeat the pattern until you feel the energy going. And now you ask, "Is there anything else?" That's saying, "I'm going to shut this line of inquiry down, unless you'd like to keep it going".

Michael Bungay Stanier is the author of seven books including *The Coaching Habit*, the best-selling book on coaching in the twenty-first century.

126

With Retrospect

Ingredients

Paper, flip chart or whiteboard

Pens

Description

From time to time, every small-business owner gets stuck. From lacking the time for strategic planning, to the fear of failure, to reaching a growth plateau, all small-business owners face challenges.

The primary objective of this technique is to assist clients in overcoming obstacles and in progressing, utilising a backward-looking approach. By constructing a comprehensive overview of past events, clients can engage in reflective analysis, comprehending the factors that have contributed to their current position. This newfound insight is then employed to formulate a strategic plan that propels them towards their desired goals. The process aims to foster momentum and facilitate the client's forward movement.

When does it work best?

This technique is useful when working with any business owner, solo or entrepreneur, but also can be just as useful for personal coaching or team coaching.

Coach and client work together to sketch a comprehensive overview of the client's business journey to date. This visual representation serves as a foundation for the coach to facilitate reflection on the significant events that have impacted the business, encompassing both positive and negative aspects. Subsequently, the coach guides the client in reviewing this map and leveraging the insights gained from their reflections, enabling them to project more effectively into the future with greater clarity and ease.

It helps them to:

1. Capture a snapshot or panoramic perspective of the significant positive and negative milestones, individuals and stakeholders that have played a role in the development of their business;
2. Take a careful, change-focused look at where they are in the present;
3. Develop a well-defined and robust growth plan that focuses on the key areas of importance, leveraging the strengths (and potential challenges) identified through the reflective overview.

Step by step

Phase 1: Paint the Picture

(Perhaps first sketch or show an example of what a finished timeline might look like.)

1. Ask the client to record the 'start' of their business on the left side of the paper or whiteboard.
2. Encourage them to draw a continuous line, mapping the highs and the lows of their business's journey with peaks and valleys respectively. It is important to ask them to create this instinctively – be clear that they should just start drawing and see where it takes them.
3. Ask them to write a brief description and an approximate date against each of the peaks and each of the troughs. For example: won first client, made first profit, moved into new office.
4. Prompt your client with questions to consider along the way. For example:
   a. What would you say were the turning points, biggest milestones, harshest disappointments, etc.?
   b. What are the things you are most proud of (big or small)?
   c. What have you been passionate about?
   d. What have you most enjoyed or most disliked?
   e. What does your business do best?
   f. What do you need to include to ensure the picture is complete and properly representative of what's happened so far?

Example:

Phase 2: Reflect – what is the map telling them?

5. Suggest to the client that the map now belongs to someone else. Ask, what do you think about that business as you look at the map?
6. What do you notice reflected in the important events?
7. Then move back to the map being theirs and explore the following questions:
   a. When/what risks did you take?
   b. How did you overcome obstacles?
   c. When/what were the best decisions and why?
   d. When/what were the worst decisions and why?
   e. What would you change about this map if you could?
   f. Do you recognise any patterns?
   g. How might you be holding onto the past?
   h. Where are you going in the future?

Phase 3: Exploring the future

8. Tell the client that you would like to explore with them what they think this map will look like if they were to project it 20 years into the future.
9. Using a fresh piece of paper, ask them to draw their 'Future Map', detailing the ups and downs of their business over the next 20 years.
   a. What do they notice?
   b. Who do they need to be to achieve this?

Maggie Grieve is an accredited leadership and team development coach, consultant and facilitator with 30 years of working with organisations and leaders across the world. She owns her own business, Ping Thinking, and is an external coach for NHS England.

Adair's 'Bubbles'

Ingredients

Pen and paper or a pre-prepared graphic.

When does it work best?

The model can be helpful for clients in leadership roles or in organisations that they perceive as dysfunctional. The model is useful for helping clients make sense of their situation and perhaps identify where they should focus their energies; or it can help to provide a vocabulary for discussion with the client's leaders and managers.

The model can also be used in team coaching to help a team make sense of its situation, perhaps discussing and agreeing on team needs and ground rules.

Description

John Adair's simple leadership model focuses on task, team and individual needs (Adair, 1973). A coach can use this model very flexibly to help a client reflect on their situation in an organisation, to consider their own or others' leadership, or to focus on their priorities. The model is also helpful as individuals or organisations navigate through change, as it helps people to consider tensions between people and tasks, group norms and individual needs.

John Adair's model is of three overlapping circles, which represent the needs of the task, the team and the individual. The task needs the team, as more than one person is required to achieve it.

The three circles interact. If the task needs are met, the effect may well flow into the team circle creating a feeling of success, fulfilment and possibly increased group unity and cohesion. The individual circle may also be influenced as individuals might feel more motivated as a result of task completion and the social connection from the team's success.

Conversely, if the needs of one of the circles are not met, the other circles will likely be affected. For example, if the individual's needs are not recognised or met, they may withdraw their cooperation or become disruptive in the group, affecting cohesion, dynamics and effectiveness, which again affects the likelihood of successful task completion.

Adair suggests that leaders need to consider the three circles and are responsible for achieving the common task, building and maintaining the team, as well as developing the individual as much as possible, given the circumstances that they are working in. The leader can be described as needing to take a 'helicopter view' over the three circles, working out where their input is required.

Step by step

1. Explain the model to the client using a diagram of the overlapping circles, explaining task, team and individual needs, and how they affect each other.
2. Allow the client to reflect on their situation, taking each circle in turn.
3. Explore the role of the leader in achieving the common task, building and maintaining the team, as well as developing the individual.
4. Invite the client to generate ideas about possible options for intervening in each circle and consider the potential effects.
5. Invite the client to use the model in their workplace for discussion with others or reflection.

Reference

Adair, J.E. (1973) *Action-Centred Leadership*. New York: McGraw-Hill.

Dave Crome is an accredited coach, consultant and Action-Centred Leadership trainer.

Behavioural Experiments – For Embedding Change

Ingredients

Paper and pen

Optional:
pre-prepared tables
or pictures to hold up
(helpful if working
online)

Description

Behavioural experiments are used in cognitive behavioural coaching (CBC) to help clients test out new ways of thinking or working, or to observe the effect of new behaviours or actions. Behavioural experiments help clients to hold themselves to account, and increase the likelihood of making a change stick.

Behavioural experiments work on the premise that behaviour and emotions are driven by internal beliefs about oneself and the world, and those beliefs in turn are shaped by experiences. If we have a bad experience with giving a presentation, for example, it might lead us to believe we are bad at presentations and make us avoid presentations in the future, or cause us to dry up or get very nervous if we have to do one. The converse is also true – if we have a good experience doing something, it makes us more likely to repeat the action, because we have positive thoughts about it.

Changing a habit can feel like stretching an elastic band – it can be achieved with some effort but there is resistance and a strong pull back towards the status quo. Resisting this pull is hard, particularly in times of stress. Behavioural experiments help clients take a systematic approach to practising a new behaviour and building commitment to it. The more we walk along a path, the more we tread down the grass. It's the same in the brain – we need to practise something for it to become the new normal.

In a behavioural experiment, the coach and client co-design a plan for the client to try out a new behaviour or action after the session and gather data to help inform their next steps. They might bring the results back to the next coaching session, or use the experiment as a tool to self-coach. How you co-design the experiment is flexible and is best when client-led.

The following is an example of a behavioural experiment for a client who has limiting beliefs about an issue, with some example answers:

When does it work best?

This tool works best for clients who are happy to do work outside the session. It suits clients who like an evidence-based approach and who respond to psycho-education. It can be helpful to suggest it when you notice a client struggling to complete the actions they commit to between coaching sessions. It can be used to boost motivation, reduce procrastination and increase confidence. A modified approach is helpful to use in team-coaching scenarios to generate team behaviour change or when the team wants to build a culture of continuous improvement or innovate quickly.

*Behavioural
Experiments –
For Embedding
Change*

Prediction	Experiment	Results	Learning
What do you assume will happen in a particular situation?	*How could you test your prediction out?*	*Record what actually happened.*	*Did your prediction come true? What can you draw from the results? What are your next steps?*
I will dry up in presentations.	I will volunteer to do two presentations, prepare as best I can and see what happens.	One actually went well. I made some mistakes the second time but no one seemed to notice.	I was not 100% right in my predictions. I am still worried about doing presentations but I need to take each one as it comes because I can do them.

The following is a more detailed example of an experiment to help a client develop a new habit. The client observes what happens and notes it down, thereby generating 'data' or an 'evidence base' for the habit or action. It is hard to notice small differences unless we pay detailed attention to them.

Note: This is an experiment, so if the client notices an action is working, the evidence they gather will help them be more motivated to repeat it. If it is not working, they can stop and try something else without having wasted too much time and energy on it. It is low risk!

What I will do: Build mindfulness into my week by stopping for 15 minutes every weekday lunchtime to use my meditation app. This experiment will last two weeks.

Stress level at work score at the beginning (1–10, where 1 is low): 9

Day	Completed? (yes/no)	Comments e.g. How it made me feel, how easy it was to do it, barriers and enablers
Monday	Yes	I felt motivated and I felt better afterwards.
Tuesday	Yes	I was motivated but found it hard to concentrate today as I had a deadline looming.
Wednesday	No	Had an urgent meeting.
Thursday	No	Forgot
Friday	Yes	I had the day off so it was easier.
Monday	No	Forgot.
Tuesday	No	Forgot. This is not going to work.
Wednesday		
Thursday		
Friday		

Stress level at work score at the end (1–10): 7

Learning and next steps: The meditation itself helped but I could not get into the habit of doing it in the middle of the working day, so I abandoned the experiment. I'm going to try again, this time doing the mindfulness at the beginning or end of the day, and I'm going to try to do it three times a week for 20 minutes instead of every day.

Step by step

Introduce the concept of cognitive behavioural approaches and explain what behaviour experiments are. Ask them if they would like to try one. If the aim is to help a client challenge limiting beliefs, you might introduce the idea in the main part of a session. If the aim is to encourage uptake of a new habit, you might introduce it towards the end.

1. Ask "How could we test out your idea/hypothesis?", "What experiment could we set up to see if that assumption is true?" or "What plan could we draw up for you to practise that action and to see whether it works for you or not?" You may have to give them some ideas – show them a template such as the one above or start them off.
2. Co-create the experiment with them, adding columns or rows where needed. It is a little easier to do this face-to-face as you can draw it out freehand, but it works well online if you have a few templates up your sleeve and can edit them in real time to suit the client. Alternatively, you can just hold up a picture and ask them to draw one out themselves.
3. Make sure they write down the purpose of their experiment and introduce a before-and-after scoring system. Add a space for them to reflect on it once they're done and to consider how they will take forward any learning from the experience
4. Agree with them how long they will do the experiment for and when you will follow up with each other.
5. You can wrap some motivational interviewing techniques around this, to ensure they are committed to the experiment. For example, asking them to score their commitment 1–10, explore barriers they might envisage in completing the experiment and how they could get support from others.

Reference

Kennerley, H., et al. (2016) *An Introduction to Cognitive Behaviour Therapy: Skills and Applications* (3rd edition). London: Sage.

Catherine Wilton is a coach, supervisor and leadership development specialist with over 20 years' experience of supporting individuals and groups. She is Director of the NHS Leadership for Personalised Care programme and Collaborative Leadership Academy.

Managing Resistance and Rupture in Supervision

Ingredients

Space for dialogue

When does it work best?

Resistance is best addressed as early as possible. Once a rupture has occurred, resolution should still be sought and if resolved can lead to a strengthened working alliance. The tool works best when both parties are prepared to become curious as to why the issues are occurring and both still funda- mentally seek a better under- standing of events.

Description

The supervisory relationship is a dynamic and unfolding process with a diverse range of influences from the supervisor, supervisee and the interaction between them. A relationship established effectively at the outset will not necessarily remain that way for the duration of any supervision contract. Sources of resistance may emanate from the supervisor as well as the supervisee. Difficulties in the working relationship can be reframed so that both parties become curious as to the reasons for the resistance rather than engaging in a battle of wills. This tool enables practitioners to unearth tacit beliefs and emotional and behavioural responses necessary to the resolution of resistance or rupture. The aim is to shift the dialogue from a reactive position towards one of reflection, neutrality and curiosity.

Step by step

1. The supervisor should aim to maintain moment-to-moment self-awareness of their subjective experience.
2. As they do so, they should attend to their own emotions, cognitions and reactions, and seek to formulate what is occurring.
3. In the service of this aim (adapting Shohet, 2012), the following questions can be a useful guide in the early stages of any resistance:
   - Is the irritation a signal that a belief about what should or should not happen in supervision has been activated?
   - What, in your own behaviour, may be reflected in the supervisee's reaction?
   - What positive commitment to exploration or change might underpin the resistance?
   - How might the supervisee's resistance be a way to help them move through the discomfort and find the courage to go forward?
   - Can I explore with the supervisee how they might be able to redirect the energy?
   - If I am stuck in understanding this, could I take this to my own super- visor to gain an outside perspective?
4. Beyond this stage of resistance, the supervisor can hold responsibility for de-escalating and working towards restoring a productive alliance. In doing so, they might consider their objectives, the perspective that underpins them and the process that enables progress (Corrie and Lane, 2015).
5. Future courses of action (adapting the work of Hersted and Gergen, 2012) might include the following options in the table.

Table: Purpose, Perspective and Process for De-escalating Ruptures in Supervision

Purpose	Perspective	Process
De-construct the realities	Most conflict results from differing interpretations of reality. The challenge is for both participants to recognise that their way of seeing is but one of multiple perspectives rather than 'the truth'.	Ask each person to tell the story from the other's point of view, enquire into possible doubts each has about their own account or bring others into the story.
De-polarise the differences	In addition to the hardening of perspectives that conflict generates, differences also become polarised.	Each consider some potential benefits in the opponent's view and seek acknowledgement from each other that there are different interpretations of the same event.
Search for commonalities	One of the most useful ways to address conflict is to search for commonalities; that is, aspects on which the different parties agree.	The supervisor and supervisee take turns to identify shared goals, values or outcomes they see in the way they are working together.
Avoid using power	If as the supervisor you adopt the position of ruling on disagreements, you are likely to cause alienation. Seek to reflect on how power appears to the other.	Ask each party to reflect on the process and seek commonalities in order to avoid resentments going 'underground'.
Focus on the 'we'	Conflict often arises as a result of people's participation in differing social traditions. Trainees, for example, are not yet part of the tradition of the supervisor or professional service provider. If the supervisor adopts the power position, the trainee is likely to comply with, but not necessarily embrace, the core values and traditions of the profession.	Here, the supervisor might focus on the 'we' (that is, what we are trying to achieve together) and the process of relating (how we can give meaning to our conversations). Through this process, supervisor and supervisee can come to share a professional tradition and professional identity.

© 2022 David A. Lane and Sarah Corrie

References

Corrie, S., and Lane, D.A. (2015) *CBT Supervision*. London: Sage.

Hersted, L., and Gergen, K.J. (2012) *Relational Leading: Practices for Dialogically Based Collaboration*. Chagrin Falls: Taos Institute.

Shohet, R. (2012) Listening to Resistance. In D. Owen and R. Shohet (eds), *Clinical Supervision in the Medical Profession*, pp.143–156. Maidenhead, Berkshire: Open University Press.

David A. Lane is the co-founder of PDF and has been involved in coaching and supervision for a number of decades. He also teaches and supervises coaches.

Sarah Corrie is a chartered coaching psychologist and runs her own coaching company, as well as supervising and training coaches and other professional groups.

Channelling Alice (for One-to-one Coaching)

Ingredients

None

When does it work best?

This tool may resonate more strongly with women, especially those who have read the book or seen the film when young, though it can work with any client of any gender when they have self-confidence issues.

Description

This model is used in one-to-one coaching to evoke confidence in those that say they lack it. The particular focus of this tool is on identity and values as a way to help bring alignment between the client's neurological levels, building out from identity and values to their behaviours and the environment around them. When these levels are aligned, clients can gain more contentedness and authenticity and consequently more self-confidence.

This coaching tool uses the world-famous novel *Alice's Adventures in Wonderland* by Lewis Carroll, which has been made into numerous films. It works best when clients feel that they are lacking in self-confidence or have lost their former confidence, and that this is holding them back either in the workplace or in life in general.

Step by step

1. Ask the client whether they have read the novel *Alice's Adventures in Wonderland* (or seen any of the films).
2. a) If they have read the novel, ask them to think about some of the characters in it and describe them.
   b) If they have not read the novel, explain some of the characters briefly to your client: the Cheshire Cat, who comes and goes; the Mad Hatter, who repeats the same stories over and over; the Queen of Hearts, who shouts orders and asks for beheadings at almost every moment; the White Rabbit, who Alice follows into Wonderland and who mistakes Alice for someone else; the Caterpillar, who appears to be smoking some sort of hallucinogenic substance and asks Alice a number of difficult questions.
3. Ask the client whether these characters (or others) bear any likeness, in their actions, no matter how small, to those around them.
   - Which friends or colleagues come and go, smiling and positive, like the Cheshire Cat?
   - Who are the people they know who seem to have the same (apparently pointless) conversation over and over again, like the Mad Hatter?
   - Who in their lives is closest to the bullying Queen of Hearts?
   - Who are they tempted to follow, as Alice followed the White Rabbit, and what is the curiosity that makes them do so?
   - And what are the difficult questions that make their heads ache, like those asked by the Caterpillar?

Channelling Alice (for One-to-one Coaching)

4. Note how in the book Alice is at first bemused, fearful and unsure of herself. But then she draws on what she herself knows to be right for her – her own sense of her identity and her own values concerning what is right and wrong. Ask your client: what is their identity made up of? What are their values and beliefs?

5. Once Alice draws on these, she finds herself at ease with all the other characters because she is content in being truly herself – her best self. She finds herself enjoying being in Wonderland and, as a result, is respected by the other characters.

6. Challenge your client to channel Alice to be their own best self. With that, they can attain self-confidence.

Jonathan Drew MBE FRCP Edin is a leadership, career and team coach and a former British ambassador and ICF UK Chapter vice president.

Back of the Envelope

Ingredients

A standard-sized envelope

A pen

When does it work best?

This technique is useful for simplifying what appears at first glance to be a complex set of circumstances or a situation with many associated factors that the client is finding overwhelming.

It can help a client when they have too many ideas about what to do or have too much information to digest and distil their issue. Ideally, this would be used during the Options and or Will phases of GROW, but it is also useful as a tool to create a succinct view of their Reality.

Description

This is a pen-and-paper activity. The underlying idea is that the envelope has limited space so the client will have to be selective about their ideas and present them succinctly.

In the natural sciences, 'back-of-the-envelope' calculation is often associated with one of the greatest physicists of the twentieth century, Enrico Fermi, who gained a reputation for getting quick and accurate answers to seemingly huge calculation problems in the scientific field that would stump other people. He did this using simple back-of-the-envelope calculations. Fermi's back-of-the-envelope problems were meant to be solved quickly – with little data and some good analytic reasoning.

Step by step

1. Give your client an envelope and pen and invite them to write notes on the back of it as you discuss the options available to them. The idea is that they use only the space on the envelope to 'draw up' their ideas and plan.
2. Do not given them any more instruction than this. The envelope has areas marked out already, due to its construction, which will help your client to separate out ideas in their own way and it has limited space, which will encourage your client to limit their ideas and include only the most relevant information.
3. Structure a coaching conversation exploring the topic through questioning as normal, but continuing to encourage the client to use only the envelope as their action plan takeaway.

Reference

Van Niewerburgh, C. (2014) *An Introduction to Coaching Skills: A Practical Guide*. London: Sage.

Maggie Grieve is an accredited leadership and team development coach, consultant and facilitator with 30 years of working with organisations and leaders across the world. She owns her own business, Ping Thinking, and is an external coach for NHS England.

COACH State

Ingredients

None

When does it work best?

The COACH state is relevant when generativity is needed and the goal is expressed as an intention rather than a destination – for example, in the case of rapid growth in a new area, in a crisis where what has worked before will no longer work or in a high-risk transition.

Unlike techniques such as guided meditations or mindfulness practices, this tool works best when applied face-to-face, as generative coaching aims to create a shared state of resonance (field) between coach and client beyond the verbal and cognitive mind, where creative ideas can easily emerge.

Description

The COACH state is a key component and technique used in Generative Change, which is a large body of work developed by Robert Dilts and Stephen Gilligan (2021). They see it as the third generation of change work, adding to traditional therapy and traditional coaching. Generative Change has three tracks: Generative Trance, Generative Coaching and Generative Consulting. All three require the individual, group or system to be in a state and relationship that are generative, where generativity is a special type of creativity that consists in conversations between the quantum world, the infinite field of possibilities and the conscious classical world. And as creativity is a function of the state of the somatic, cognitive and relational filters or biases, Generative Change work requires keeping a balance between a relaxed readiness in the body and focused spaciousness in the mind.

All three types of Generative Change work use a flexible six-step model in which the organising principle is creativity. In Generative Coaching, the first step is to open a relational COACH field and be in a psychologically necessary COACH state.

COACH is an acronym for:
- CENTRED in the body, especially the belly centre
- OPEN to possibilities, in the heart and mind, from the centre
- AWARE and awake to oneself and one's filters, as well as to the others around
- CONNECTED to one's resources and intelligence, as well as to the bigger system
- HOLDING and welcoming all that is happening with curiosity and resourcefulness.

Highlights:
- The opposite of COACH is CRASH (Contracted, Reactive, Analysis paralysis, Separated, Hostile/Hurting/Hating). Another name is 'neuro-muscular lock', where the only possible responses are fight, flight, freeze or fold (collapse).
- Dilts and Gilligan consider the true COACH state to be that of equanimity, as Buddhists call it (i.e. a balanced mental state, independent of emotions or feelings whether they are joy, sadness, frustration or even anger). This is because a COACH state is a function of somatic, cognitive and relational filters specific to each person.
- The COACH-state level varies during a session. Dilts and Gilligan recommend that it is at an optimum between 7 and 10, with 10 being the maximum. Self-scaling helps to identify the level. If in CRASH, it is advised to first slow down, pause and breathe, before centring and reactivating the COACH state.

COACH State

- Regular practice of the COACH state outside coaching enables the client to build an anchor accessible under all conditions. It becomes an automatic unconscious skill and awareness, and a way of life.

Step by step

Through informal discussion, the coach can find out what works for the client by asking how they get into their best possible state and access their inner resources. Answers such as yoga, walking in the forest or singing provide useful information. They help the coach choose relevant metaphorical activities that can be integrated into the following step-by-step process, which is only a guide and outlines what you might say to a client. More detailed instructions can be provided when it comes to the bodily experience.

1. Sit or stand in a comfortable position with both feet flat on the floor and the spine erect. Make sure that breathing is regular and comes from the belly.
2. Bring your attention to the soles of your feet. Become aware of the universe of sensations in the bottom of your feet.
3. Expand your awareness to the physical volume of your feet and gradually move it to your hips, your belly centre. Breathe deeply into it and say "I am here, I am present, I am centred".
   NB: The physical centre of a body is a powerful energy area located towards the belly. It can easily be found by crossing one leg over the other while standing, or by performing a static or dynamic movement to find balance. Repeat the movement three times, for the benefits of the body and the mind.
4. Stay aware of your lower body and expand your awareness though your upper body and organs, gradually to your chest. Bring awareness to your heart centre, breathe into your chest and say "I am open, I am opening".
   NB: The accompanying movement can consist of raising the arms to the sky while standing on tiptoes. Return to the normal position, repeat the sequence three times.
5. Continue to expand your awareness up gradually through your upper limbs and body, to the face. Include all the senses in the head. Breathe in your head centre and say, "I am awake, I am aware, I am clear and alert".
6. Staying in contact with your body and all three centres (belly, heart, head), become aware of all the space below you to the centre of the earth, above you to the sky, to your left and right, behind and in front of you. Feel a deep sense of connection to your feet, the three centres, the environment. Be aware of your inner resources and those in the field around you. When you can experience a connection, say "I am connected".
7. Keeping your awareness on your body and simultaneously on the space around you, sense a type of field in which you can hold all the resources, strengths, intelligence and wisdom available to you as well as disturbing energies such as fear, anger and sadness. Feel the sense of courage and

COACH State

confidence to face whatever comes as you stay centred and present and open. Say to yourself, "I am ready, I can hold whatever is here with curiosity, resourcefulness and creativity".

The whole sequence above can be performed in a slow Tai Chi movement while saying, "I am centred, I am open, I am alert and awake, I am connected, I am holding the space".

References

Dilts, R. (2023) The COACH State. Available from: https://www.youtube.com/watch?v=GSgn45pfeYg [Retrieved 25 April 2023].

Dilts, R., and Gilligan, S. (2021) *Generative Coaching Volume 1: The Journey of Creative and Sustainable Change*. The International Association for Generative Change.

Francoise Orlov is an accredited master coach, mentor and coach supervisor working internationally with leaders, teams, boards and executive coaches across industries.

Being the Observer

Ingredients

A quiet space

When does it work best?

The tool works best when clients are wrapped up in their own world, do not have time for reflection, are self-obsessed or spend considerable periods ruminating about past events or worrying about future events, when their energies could be better directed towards current tasks and a here-and-now focus.

Reference

Passmore, J. (2018) Mindfulness Coaching Techniques: Being the Observer. *The Coaching Psychologist*, 14(2): 105–107.

Jonathan Passmore is a chartered psychologist, accredited master executive coach, team coach, supervisor, author and professor at Henley Business School.

Description

Much of our life is spent rushing between one task and the next. We are so engaged in the process that we rarely take time to observe what is happening around us, or to observe ourselves. When things become difficult, we can find ourselves worrying about past or future events, ruminating about such events and how we dealt with them or might deal with them.

This exercise is designed to be used with coaching clients to help them observe their behaviour, their thoughts and their feelings. By doing so, we are encouraging our clients to become more self-aware. The exercise is particularly useful for clients when they perceive something has gone wrong, or has not gone as they would have liked. By helping our clients to step out from their thought-stream or rumination about a past event, we can help them to take a more objective perspective of events, observe themselves and make choices about thought, feelings and behaviours which may be more helpful. As with most of these exercises, they can be taught or shared with clients quickly and used as homework or activities between sessions, with the following coaching session used to explore observations, insights and learning.

Step by step

1. If a client talks about an issue that has been troubling them, and the thought or anxiety is recurring, invite them to notice when this thought occurs.
2. Invite them to take five minutes for a mindfulness task by taking a few breaths and observing their body as they sit in the chair.
3. As they engage in the mindfulness task, invite them to be aware of any sensations in their body – to observe them but not to judge these sensations.
4. Next, invite them to imagine they are in a movie theatre and are watching their thoughts as if they were a movie.
5. Help them to see their thoughts as separate from themselves – as opposed to *being* them – and to simply watch the 'movie'.
6. If the 'movie' gets too difficult, suggest they turn their attention back to their breathing.
7. When ready, they should return to the 'movie'.
8. Encourage them to simply watch the 'movie' without analysing or judging.
9. At the end of the task, ask the client whether, as they sat with the 'movie', it changed – and if so, what changed?
10. Explore with the client if there is an alternative 'movie' about the same story that they could 'play'. What would this be?
11. Help them to recognise that our thoughts are not the truth, but a subjective experience.

The Thought Train Metaphor

Ingredients

None

When does it work best?

The metaphor is particularly useful to use when clients are unhelpfully caught up in repetitive thoughts, excessively worrying, and are unaware of this process. It can be introduced as a method to help them build awareness of their thought process, to become more choiceful in how they respond to different thoughts, rather than simply resorting to automatic reactions.

Description

This metaphor is designed to highlight the often-repetitive nature of our mind as it continually delivers thoughts into our awareness. The metaphor describes a train that travels around a track, pulling a variety of carriages. The train is like our minds and the carriages are like our thoughts; some carriages we instinctively like and some we don't like, just like our thoughts. We can end up habitually pushing away the thoughts that we don't like or clinging to the thoughts we do like. This can interfere with the flow of thoughts and distract us from our task at hand.

By making the comparison between a train and our mind, the metaphor helps us to see our thinking process and our habitual responses to thoughts with more observational distance. This sets the scene for mindful acceptance as a more helpful alternative.

Step by step

1. Invite the client to bring a recent example of when they were caught up in a repetitive, unhelpful thought cycle. Then, introduce them to the following metaphor (if possible, have a toy train to hand, or a video of one on your phone, to bring the metaphor alive).
2. "Imagine this train and all its carriages are a little bit like your mind. The train comes and goes around the track and in and out of the station 24/7. Some of the carriages you might prefer, like the engine at the front that does all the hard work. And some you don't like so much, like the caboose at the back that's heavy and drags things down. It can be tempting to interfere with the train to focus on the carriages you like and get rid of the ones you don't."
3. "But if you start doing this too much, you can stop the train working smoothly."
4. "And isn't your mind a little like that too? Delivering thoughts to you that come and go 24/7. Some you like and you end up clinging to them because they make you feel good. Some you don't like and you want to get rid of them. And so we end up responding to them differently."
5. "The trick is learning to treat our thoughts broadly the same and to cultivate a healthy relationship to them."
6. "Just like the train, we sit back and observe them without automatically getting pulled into either clinging to them or pushing them away."
7. "That way, we can focus on what is important to us."

Dr Joe Oliver is a consultant clinical psychologist, founder of Contextual Consulting and an associate professor at UCL.

Real-play

Ingredients

None

Description

Play is often overlooked as a crucial element in adult learning and development. It can aid in the re-evaluation of role expectations, facilitate negotiations between claimed and granted identities, and help navigate between existing ego structures, future selves and role transitions, all while providing a safe and non-threatening environment.

Real-play is an experiential coaching intervention that uses improvisation and simulation to help clients practise and refine their skills in a safe and supportive environment. It draws on concepts from psychodrama, a therapeutic approach developed by Jacob Levy Moreno in the 1920s that emphasises the use of drama, action methods and role playing to help individuals gain a deeper understanding of their emotions and behaviours and explore different perspectives on their issues in a safe and supportive environment.

Real-play is designed to help clients develop both cognitive and affective soft skills, such as communication, empathy, problem solving and emotional regulation. It is therefore effective in building clients' confidence and self-efficacy, which can lead to increased motivation and learning goal orientation.

When does it work best?

Real-play is a powerful coaching intervention tool for developing soft skills that are challenging to master through traditional training methods. This approach is particularly effective when clients can practise in an immersive environment, reflect on the experience and receive observations from their coach and peers (when team coaching). Real-play is ideal for tackling specific challenges or scenarios that clients may face in their personal or professional lives. It provides a deeper understanding of complex issues and can help leaders develop new management or communication skills. Furthermore, in team coaching, team members can learn to appreciate each other's perspectives, promoting a more collaborative work environment. Real-play can also be used for personal growth, conflict resolution, diversity and inclusion training, and more. Its versatility makes it an indispensable coaching tool for various contexts and situations.

Real-play

Step by step

1. Create a supportive and safe environment for the client before the Real-play intervention.
2. Begin with a warm-up activity to facilitate a successful Real-play intervention. This can be a game or exercise that invokes a playful mindset in the client, helping them respond spontaneously and authentically to the situation at hand.
3. Obtain a brief overview of the client's specific situation and the key issues involved.
4. Identify the soft skills that the client wants to develop and how they believe it may benefit their proximal and distal coaching goals.
5. Ask the client to create a simple duologue scenario or simulation that allows them as the protagonist to practise their desired skills, including the characteristics and motivations of the person the coach is to 'play' as the second interlocutor (the antagonist). Alternatively, a professional role player or actor may be used.
6. Conduct Real-play, then offer the client space and time to reflect on their experiences to gain insight into not only their own behaviour (as the protagonist) but also that of the second interlocutor (the antagonist).
7. Debrief the Real-play through open-ended questions and prompts, such as asking what worked well and what could be improved, and by developing a plan for further soft skills practise and development.
8. Offer feedback to the client from the perspective of playing the second interlocutor. If team coaching, team members as observers may also share their observations with the client.

References

Erikson, E.H. (1993) *Childhood and Society.* W.W. Norton & Company.

Moreno, J.L., and Moreno, Z.T. (1975) *Psychodrama, Vol. 3.* Beacon, NY: Beacon House.

Moreno, Z.T., Horvatin, T., and Schreiber, E. (2015) *The Quintessential Zerka: Writings by Zerka Toeman Moreno on Psychodrama, Sociometry and Group Psychotherapy.*

Passmore, J. (2014) *Mastery in Coaching: A Complete Psychological Toolkit for Advanced Coaching.* Kogan Page.

Callum O'Neill is a BPS registered psychologist and ICF accredited coach (PCC).

Director's Chair

Ingredients

Any chair that differs from the ones used by the coach and client

When does it work best?

This is most helpful during one-to-one coaching between the Reality and the Options stages of GROW. It is particularly useful if the topic being discussed concerns relationships between multiple people or individuals.

Reference

Van Niewerburgh, C. (2014) *An Introduction to Coaching Skills: A Practical Guide*. London: Sage.

Claudia Day is a coach and entrepreneur, co-founder of My Coaching Place, part of the AC UK leadership team, and holds a master's in coaching and behavioural change (Henley) and a master's in business administration (MIT).

Description

The Director's Chair is an exercise where the client has to imagine creating and directing a play about their own life. The role of the director allows the client to step out of their own shoes and see themselves from another position. This helps them to gain a different perspective of the situation they are facing and explore solutions. This tool also allows the client to distance themselves from the challenge and come up with creative solutions by practising or acting out ideas to get a further sense of the impact of putting their ideas into practice.

Step by step

1. After allowing some silence and getting some signal that the client is stuck or very centred on a single perspective, offer to try an exercise that might help – if they would like.
2. If they say yes, set the scene by describing to the client that they will be directing a play about their own life, set in the present time. Explain that the plot will be the summary of their 'reality'.
3. Set up the extra chair as the director's chair and invite the client to get into the director role. (If working remotely, you can ask the client to bring themselves another chair and to sit on that.)
4. Ask the director how they would select the person to play themselves (the leading role). How would they find the right actor to play the lead character? What will they be looking for as the director? What need to be the strengths of that character?
5. Ask the director to briefly outline the plot as if talking to the actors of the play. The client can stand up and show the characters how the director would like them to perform their roles. For this part, the coach can suggest acting out extremes to understand how the situation would play out. For example, if the main actor plays their character extra empathetically, what impact would this have on the plot?
6. All along, the coach can ask questions to gain a better understanding of the various roles and how the director sees them.
7. Finally, the director is asked to give advice to the lead-role actor about how they can deal with the situation facing them.

Director's Chair

Team Evolution

Ingredients

Copy of the 'Team Performance Curve'

Copies of 'The Five Stages of Team Performance' (one for each participant)

Large open room if possible

Description

The Team Evolution technique helps clients who wish to create team change. It's a creative way of grappling with opportunities or obstacles where a team is experiencing a challenging environment. It uses a J curve to help the team represent their current situation and their potential, and to go on to jointly create a plan that moves them forward. By involving the team in this structured way of thinking about their team, its performance and its capabilities, clients/leaders are able to achieve lasting change in how the team collectively feels, thinks and acts. By encouraging team members to explore the Team Performance Curve together, the team as a whole is able to define current and future desired performance and create plans that will take them towards those desired goals and embed the changes required.

The Team Performance Curve is informed by the work of Jon Katzenbach and Douglas Smith (1993). Katzenbach and Smith define a team as "a small group of people with complementary skills who are committed to a common purpose, performance goals and approach for which they are mutually accountable". This definition differentiates teams from groups, placing an emphasis on the key ingredients of shared purpose, goals and approach as well as the mutual accountability element. They suggested five levels of teamwork, which could be plotted on an X–Y axis to form a J-shaped curve. The steps outlined below will help underpin a coaching conversation with a team about where they are now and what they need to do to evolve.

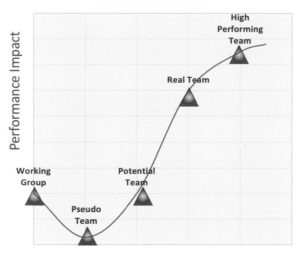

Team Effectiveness

The Five Stages of Team Performance

1. Working group

This is not a team; rather, it is a group of individuals whose outputs rely on the sum of 'individual bests'. Members don't pursue collective outputs that require joint effort and they take responsibility only for their own individual results. They interact primarily to share information and practices that enable them to act within their own individual sphere of responsibility.

2. Pseudo team

This team isn't focused on achieving collective performance and isn't looking to shape a common purpose or performance goals together. They may call themselves a team, but these are the weakest of all groups, in terms of their combined impact on performance. In these teams, the whole is less than the sum of the individual parts, working separately. This results in suboptimal performance and an unhealthy and unproductive environment. For those familiar with the work of Tuckman (1965), this stage is also referred to as the 'storming' stage of team development. They do have a significant, incremental performance need or opportunity, and to develop potential this pseudo team must define their goal(s) so there is something identifiable and valuable to the organisation that they can achieve as a team together. Teams stuck here should also focus on how team members can individually and collectively contribute towards these identified goals.

3. Potential team

As the name suggests, this team has potential. It is moving in the right direction but hasn't yet established collective accountability, although it is trying to improve its performance impact. The team needs more clarity on purpose, goals and work products, and should develop how they will undertake and practise a common working approach. A potential team is becoming effective and is making its way up the performance axis, but still needs to develop collective accountability. Katzenbach and Smith identify the steepest performance gain between being a potential team and becoming a real team.

4. Real team

This team is composed of a small number of people with complementary skills, who are equally committed and hold themselves mutually accountable for a common purpose, goals and working approach. This is the minimum level that a leader needs to attain to ensure a successful outcome and it has the potential for a truly significant impact on overall performance.

5. High-performance team

This group meets all the conditions of the real team but they don't stop there. The members of this team are deeply committed to one another's personal development and success. This condition normally transcends the whole team. This team outperforms all other teams and even expectations. It is a powerful possibility and an excellent role model for all real and potential teams.

Team Evolution

In explaining these definitions, the coach should make the participants aware also of the need for realism. We know that, most often, teams and their members are transitory. They do not necessarily exist for long enough to achieve this level of performance and are always subject to personnel changes.

When does it work best?

This technique works best in any team situation where that team would like to develop relationships and performance. The objective is to help them to agree the characteristics they believe they share and what they think they should concentrate on to move them to where they want to be.

It can be particularly useful for taking teams and their participants away from an inward focus on what's stopping them, and into the realms of possibility. It is also effective at helping them to characterise and agree the challenges they face, and uncover opportunities to tackle these obstacles together. The discursive nature of the exercise supported by reflection and problem-solving thinking time can help teams to reframe their thinking.

The principles are applicable to all contexts of teams or groups whether simple or complex, highly agile or more predictive.

Step by step

1. Work with the team to agree some ground rules for the exercise. These should include being tactful about their current state, avoiding being personal with members of the team, agreeing not to allocate blame or fault.
2. Discuss your and their roles as coach and client, and encourage questions about this format before you start. Some of your clients may not be familiar with the coaching approach to solution-focused problem solving.
3. Show participants the Team Performance Curve and briefly discuss each phase so that participants understand the characteristics of each one.
4. Invite them first to discuss the characteristics they believe they share as a group and then to share what they think they should concentrate on to move them to where they'd like to be. Allow plenty of time for this step, using your own preferred exploratory questions, and encourage group interaction by seeking further questions from team members too. Perhaps invite questions around previous teams (good and bad) that participants have been part of or have worked alongside, and what they felt made them good or bad. You could also explore the concept of organisations they each admire and ask the team to identify where they think those companies/teams sit on the curve.
5. Draw the discussion to a gentle close and agree what's been produced, what the agreed position represents, what options exist, what problems

Team Evolution

exist and so on, so that participants can then work together to draw up a two- or three-point high-level action plan on what would move them forward. You could use the Collective Thinking tool to ensure all voices in the room are heard.

6. Finish the session with a stand-up exercise for all participants – the cocktail party – where each team member moves around the room, seeking a private one-on-one, standing conversation with everyone individually. In each conversation, they should share "What I respect about you" and "What I would like you to pay attention to". As coach, you should not participate in this session – allow them the space to carry this out on their own.

References

Katzenbach, J.R., and Smith, D.K. (1993) *The Wisdom of Teams: Creating the High-performance Organisation*. Boston: Harvard Business School.

Tuckman, B.W. (1965) Developmental Sequence in Small Groups. *Psychological Bulletin*, 63(6): 384–399.

Maggie Grieve is an accredited leadership and team development coach, consultant and facilitator with 30 years of working with organisations and leaders across the world. She owns her own business, Ping Thinking, and is an external coach for NHS England.

Comfort Zones

Ingredients

Paper and pen

When does it work best?

This is helpful when you can see that your client is stuck and doesn't think they have any tools that can help them do the thing they are afraid of. It can also be useful with teams.

Description

In order to learn and grow, people must move beyond their immediate comfort zones into an area of discomfort. For some people, it is hard to move into that zone and they can forget that they often already have tools that they can use to get there. Sometimes, the things that people are avoiding seem to them to have no links; they are just 'things to be avoided'. However, when these individual elements are grouped together, sometimes they can illuminate something bigger – it can be this combination that has become the real block for them.

Step by step

1. Ask the client to draw two overlapping circles (or provide them with a template with pre-drawn circles).

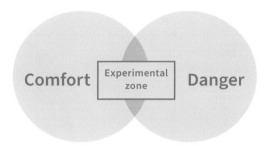

2. Invite them to start with the left-hand circle: the comfort zone. Get them to write the things that they find easy to do in the broader context of the issue you are speaking about. For example, you might be speaking about presenting.
3. Get the client to write about all the situations they find comfortable when they have to speak. It is necessary to zoom in and out here – presenting to an audience (the issue) vs. generally speaking in front of people (more broadly); or perhaps giving feedback to an individual (the issue) vs. voicing disagreement (more broadly). Once they have reflected on this, ask them to speak to you about what they have written.
4. Next, invite the client to turn to the right-hand circle: the danger zone. Get them to write down all the things that they find uncomfortable or hard to do, or which scare them about the broad issue. Again, zoom in and zoom out. Once they have finished, ask them to speak to you about what they have written.

Claire Rason is a coach, the founder of professional services, coaching-powered consultancy Client Talk and host of the podcast Lawyer's Coach.

5. Now, think about the overlap. This is the experimental zone. Are there things that they could use from their comfort zone to help move some of the things in the danger zone across into the experimental zone?

6. If you are doing this exercise with a team, you might ask the team whether there are things that people in the team find they are comfortable with that could help support others move their activities into the experimental zone.

7. Ask your client: are there any themes in what they have written down? If there are, you might want to explore these together, in whichever way you would normally do this.

Noble Certainties

Ingredients

None

Description

William Isaacs defines our 'noble certainties' as our interpretations of the world around us that blind us and limit our freedom to think and to engage in dialogue (Isaacs, 1999).

Most of the issues we help our clients to reflect on are relational, and our ability to relate well to others depends on our abilities to listen and to speak without judgement or blame. Our noble certainties get in the way of our listening and our ability to voice without prejudice.

Imagine yourself, as coach, working with a client who hasn't done what they said they would do at the end of your last session together. What thoughts go through your head? Those thoughts might include things such as:

- She's not committed
- She's not ready to be coached
- She doesn't have what it takes to be a great leader
- I'm a terrible coach.

These are our noble certainties and they get in the way of us being *really* curious as to what might actually have happened. They also show up in what we say. For example, in this case, instead of exploring what happened post the last session, I may say: "I'm not sure coaching is working for you," with a disappointed look on my face, such that the client feels compelled to defend their lack of action. We miss the opportunity to explore what happened to the client's intention, the extent to which it was fully formed, how it might have evolved in conversation with others and what else might have happened to deflect that intention.

We all have noble certainties, but few of us are fully aware of those certainties or the impact they have on our relationship with others.

Step by step

1. Ask the client to identify the most important part of the conversation and to detail exactly what was said.
2. With regard to their own voicings, invite the client to hypothesise what impact their words may have had on the other person.
3. What possible judgements do they detect behind their own voicings?
4. Frame these judgements as 'noble certainties' and invite the client to challenge the extent to which these noble certainties are objectively true.
5. Invite the client to speculate as to how these noble certainties may be impacting on other relationships.
6. What insights does the client realise about themselves, their values and their strongly held beliefs?

Noble Certainties

Next:

1. Ask the client the extent to which they felt they were fully present and listening to the other person.
2. If unsure, ask the client what the other person was really trying to say when they said "xyz". If the client appears sure they do know what the other person meant, present them with other options and ask them how they can be sure their interpretation is correct.
3. Ask the client what might have got in the way of enquiring more deeply as to what the other person was trying to say.
4. Frame these obstacles to listening as 'noble certainties' and invite the client to challenge the extent to which these noble certainties are objectively true.
5. Invite the client to speculate as to how these noble certainties may be impacting on other relationships.
6. What insights does the client realise about themselves, their values and their strongly held beliefs?

In supervision, as supervisor:

1. Ask the coach to identify the most important part of the coaching conversation and to detail exactly what was said.
2. As above, explore what noble certainties may have been at play in possibly limiting the coach's capacities to listen and to voice without prejudice or judgement.
3. What insights does the coach realise about themselves, their values and their strongly held beliefs?

Reference

Isaacs, W. (1999) *Dialogue and the Art of Thinking Together.* London: Doubleday.

Paul Lawrence is a director of the Centre for Coaching in Organisations, an author and researcher based in Australia

Keeping Track of What Takes Your Attention

Ingredients

Client note-keeping method

Notebook or phone app

When does it work best?

This approach can be useful at any time but coaches find that this strategy is very useful when you are getting to know a client and they are getting to know themselves. Clients can struggle to remember to take the notes and so don't do it. Make sure you coach them to find a strong anchor to link the process to.

Description

This is a diary and note-keeping process to gather information about what takes our attention, when, in what circumstances and under what influences. Getting off autopilot and gathering information can provide deep insight. This strategy is very useful when you are getting to know a client and they are getting to know themselves. It helps too to identify clusters of behaviours or common factors that trigger feelings and behaviours. When it comes to wellbeing and change, this matters. It is vital to have information about ourselves and how we respond to certain situations and events in our lives so that we can make different choices at those moments.

People are often unaware of these patterns, and once they begin to see them, they can plan to make choices around them in service of the change that they are seeking. There is also a balance in our awareness between what is going on externally and what is going on internally. The two are of course continually linked and knowing which is the strongest and which is the weakest matters if we are to change.

Step by step

1. Ask your client if they are willing to keep a certain kind of diary for a week and then to share that with you in your coaching. It is best to use a separate notebook (or it can be done on a device such as a phone). However the client decides to do it, the objective is to answer a few simple questions.
2. Ask the following questions one at a time and ask the client to record the question and the answer, which is to be written down in the notebook or wherever they are keeping the information for the project.
   Question 1. "What do you have your attention on right now?" In the diary they write down the answer.
3. The next question in the diary is "What are you feeling right now?" Again, they write their feelings.
4. The third question is "Who or what is here with you?" This could be anyone from parent to cat to no one. As you are doing this with them in a coaching session, they will probably write you down!
5. The last question is "What else are you noticing?" This can be something they are thinking or feeling or sensing or something that is taking place outside of themselves.
6. Request that they fill in these questions six times a day in their notebook (or other way of recording), starting when they wake up and then at the following intervals: mid-morning, lunch time, mid-afternoon, early evening and then before sleep. This is to be done before you meet for your next coaching session. A good way to assist in this is to ask them to set a phone alarm for the various times of day, to prompt them to fill it in.

From PITs to PETs: A Simple Tool for Challenging the Inner Critic

Ingredients

Paper and pen

Optional: a pre-prepared table with two columns (this is helpful if working online)

Description

From PITs to PETs is a cognitive behavioural coaching (CBC) tool that helps clients identify and challenge their inner critic, or in other words the limiting beliefs that might be getting in their way. It helps the client move from Performance Inhibiting Thoughts (PITs) to Performance Enhancing Thoughts (PETs).

CBC is based on the premise that our thoughts, behaviours, emotions and physical sensations are all linked. If the 'story' we tell ourselves is negative, we are less likely to be able to perform at our best. PITs stop us noticing any alternatives, positives or potential in a situation. Some PITs can be so strong as to put us into 'fight or flight' mode. At such times, the blood drains from the pre-frontal cortex and we are literally unable to think straight. By challenging overly negative thoughts and assumptions we can develop a more balanced view of things and become more able to overcome difficulties.

Note that 'thoughts' in CBC can be images and memories as well as actual thoughts and internal monologue.

When does it work best?

From PETs to PETs works best in one-to-one coaching, when you notice or suspect that a client may have a limiting belief that is holding them back or you have a client who is overly self-critical. It is helpful for clients dealing with stress, change or career transitions, or when they present with low confidence or self-esteem. It can also be useful when clients are feeling stuck or are procrastinating about something. It's well suited to clients who like an evidence-based approach and respond well to psycho-education.

From PITs to PETs, like many other CBC techniques, aims to increase the client's confidence, self-awareness and ability to problem solve, and encourages them to take responsibility for their actions and move forward.

Examples of PITs with corresponding examples of PETs include:

PITs	PETs
I'm terrible at writing reports.	I got criticised last time but overall I'm ok at this, even if I don't like doing it.
I'm going to mess up this speech.	If I mess up, it's not the end of the world and if I practise it's unlikely to be a disaster.
No one is going to take me seriously in this meeting.	I know my stuff and I have something important to contribute. I can prepare some points in advance that I know are important.

Step by step

1. Introduce the concept of cognitive behavioural coaching and explain the PITs and PETs acronyms. Draw out the two columns on a piece of paper (or share a template online).
2. Ask the client to identify any PITs they are having about the issue they are facing.
3. Use language that will engage them – some people engage quickly with the concept of limiting thoughts or beliefs, whereas others respond better if you refer to PITs as a narrative – for example, "What story are you telling yourself about this that isn't helpful?" Personifying the inner critic works best for some: "What are you hearing your critic say?"
4. Get them to write each PIT down, in the first person. It is sometimes best to write the first one or two for them – with their consent – until they get the hang of it.
5. To expand the conversation, ask, "What else are you telling yourself about the situation?", "What other thoughts come to mind?" or "What images/memories are emerging for you in relation to x?"
6. Once they've explored their PITs, guide them into creating some PETs for each statement. Again, they may need help to begin with – some people find it easier to do this than others and you may need to be more directive than you would normally be until they get into the flow of it.
7. For images or memories that they've identified as PITs, the idea is to come up with alternative images with more positive connotations, or to amend the images in some way. You can get them to verbalise images or to draw them out if you think a creative approach would help them reflect more deeply.

8. Once you've completed the table, wrap up the exercise with questions like "What have you learned through doing this?" and "How could this help you going forward?" Depending on the client, you might want to gauge their commitment to revisiting the list or practising the technique through scaling, or giving them the best chance of embedding the new ways of thinking they have identified by co-creating a behaviour experiment with them (see the Behavioural Experiments tool).

Reference

Neenan, M., and Palmer, S. (2001) Cognitive Behavioural Coaching. *Stress News*, 13(3): 15–18.

Catherine Wilton is a coach, supervisor and leadership development specialist with over 20 years' experience of supporting individuals and groups. She is Director of the NHS Leadership for Personalised Care programme and Collaborative Leadership Academy.

Successful Executive Landing

Ingredients

None

Description

For many reasons, especially in today and tomorrow's VUCA (volatile, uncertain, complex, ambiguous) and even BANI (brittle, anxious, non-linear, incomprehensible) world, where disruptive and transformative kinds of experience, mindsets and ways of working are needed, various organisations have a common practice of adding external executives to their internally grown leadership bench. These executives may come from different firms, industries, countries or cultural societies, with diverse backgrounds, intentions and aspirations.

However, due to many factors, the successful landing rate of externally hired executives is low. Both parties, the organisations and external executives, fail in this situation. They fail to integrate and assimilate and, even worse, many times they fail the team and business.

The good news is that organisations have developed many interventions to increase the success rate and therefore to benefit all related stakeholders and businesses. These include preparing the internal eco-system for the new executive's arrival and providing executive transition coaching.

As a seasoned Chinese executive coach, Cathleen Wu has developed and implemented a coaching tool aiming to support successful executive landing.

Step by step

Many traditional Chinese characters hold profound and multi-dimensional meanings, including 寧 (ning).

From the top to the bottom, this 寧 character consists of four independent words. Their individual meanings are 'the house', 'the heart', 'the food' and 'the children', respectively. Put together, 寧 means a stable, peaceful and meaningful status, which resonates well with ideal status of executive landing. Here below is the step-by-step process:

1. The coach can explain the multiple meanings of 寧 and how it links to new hire landing of the executive client. It can help to raise the client's willingness, openness and interest to explore and experiment during their onboarding period.
2. The coach can then invite the client to explore the topmost meaning ('the house'), which in a corporate context refers to the tangible and intangible organisational culture, structures, processes, policies and various internal and external stakeholders.

3. Following that, the coach and client come to the part meaning 'the heart'. This is where the client reflects deeper on their true intent and motivation to join the new organisation, as well as their compelling vision and future aspirations.
4. The third part is 'the food', which implies the quick understanding of the business situation, the product and service, the competitive strategy and tactics, and so forth. Here, the client must gain a quick win in order to prove themself and gain initial credibility and trust.
5. Last but for sure not least, the coach and client should talk about their team – checking the current team engagement and effectiveness levels, envisioning the desired situation and how to close the gaps by various means.

Cathleen Wu is an ICF MCC executive and leadership coach based in China.

The IMPACT Process

Ingredients

Pieces of paper and cards, each with one of the 10 Emotional Salary Barometer factors (see below) written on them

Description

The IMPACT Process is a technique to explore emotional salary (the non-financial/emotional benefits of working). This technique was designed to be used with the 10 factors of the Emotional Salary Barometer framework (Autonomy, Belonging, Creativity, Direction, Enjoyment, Inspiration, Mastery, Personal Growth, Professional Growth, Purpose) but can be used without the framework or by substituting the framework with another appropriate set of criteria.

Table: The 10 Factors of Emotional Salary

Autonomy: Freedom to manage your working style, projects and time
Belonging: Feeling connected, appreciated and valued at work
Creativity: Exploration, development and expression of original ideas
Direction: Being able to co-create a fulfilling career path
Enjoyment: Having fun and authentic social interactions at work
Inspiration: Having a sense of possibility and gaining new insights
Mastery: Working towards achieving true excellence in your work
Personal Growth: Gaining self-awareness and developing as a human being
Professional Growth: Developing your professional talents, skills and abilities
Purpose: Feeling that you are contributing to a greater purpose

When does it work best?

This technique works best when a client wants to explore their relationship with their work and gain some deeper insights. This can be because they feel dissatisfied but are struggling to articulate why, because they want to explore career development opportunities or simply to gain greater awareness into what is important to them in relation to their work.

Step by step

1. Explain the IMPACT Process to the client and explore it with them step by step.
2. **I – IDENTIFY**: Help your client to identify the emotional benefits they gain from working. Place pieces of paper, each with one of the 10 factors written on it, on the floor. (If you are working virtually with your client, ask them to write down the 10 factors of emotional salary on a piece of paper.)
3. Ask the client to move to the first factor and give it a score out of 10 in terms of how much of that factor they perceive they have (with 10 being the highest).
4. Repeat with the remaining factors.
5. Ask the client to rank the factors in terms of their importance to them as an individual.

6. **M – MISSING**: Explore with the client which factors are currently missing and would like to focus on increasing.
7. **P – PROACTIVELY:** Encourage them to think about which opportunities exist for them to increase these missing factors.
8. **A: ACTIONS:** Explore with the client what actions or decisions they might need to take in order to increase the missing factors.
9. **C: CONVERSATIONS:** Help your client to identify what conversations need to take place to facilitate this.
10. **T: TAKE RESPONSIBILITY:** Encourage the client to commit to a time for the action/conversation.

Clodagh Beaty is a leadership and organisational development specialist and coach and co-creator of the Emotional Salary Barometer.

AI-generated Artwork

Ingredients

Device with an internet connection and a browser (e.g. laptop, smartphone, tablet)

When does it work best?

This can be helpful when working with clients in a digital coaching environment and who have a big appetite for innovation, and also for those who are feeling stuck in their thinking. When rational analysis of a situation isn't getting far, this technique might spark new solutions into life. It's particularly helpful when working with clients who say that they'd like to do something creative but that they don't have the natural creative ability to work with art supplies.

Description

Sometimes the linear, rational parts of our minds can take control of thinking, limiting our ability to think abstractly and solve problems creatively (McGilchrist, 2019). By intentionally introducing divergent thinking into a coaching session, we can support our clients in bringing balance to their convergent thinking, unlocking new possibilities. This could look like representing a coaching topic in the form of an image on a postcard, describing it as a metaphor, using art supplies to create something entirely new or introducing toys and small objects onto a table. We can use technology to dynamically produce a brand-new image based on a prompt from the clients (such as "I need to get better at time management"), powered by deep-learning artificial intelligence. This always catalyses something different in a coaching session, activating different parts of the brain, and increasing how memorable the coaching time is.

Step by step

1. Between coaching sessions, find an AI artwork-generation tool. Two free and simple to use examples are Stable Diffusion (Diffusion, 2022) and WOMBO Dream (Dream, 2022).
2. During the session, the coach can load the page of the tool, and either share their screen or send the link to their client.
3. Allow the client to define a text prompt for the artwork, and type this into the prompt field.
4. If required (depending on the tool selected), work with the client to define any other inputs (some will ask for art style, others may have configurable quality settings).
5. When the artwork has been created, invite the client to describe the image.
6. Invite the client to consider what meaning they are taking from the image, based on their original coaching topic.
7. Adopting a curious approach continue the conversation, probing further into the image and the client's topic as appropriate.
8. Before concluding the coaching session, offer the client the chance to save their image, in case they'd like to keep it for future reference and reflection.

References

Diffusion (2022) Available from: https://stablediffusionweb.com/.

Dream (2022) Available from: https://dream.ai/.

McGilchrist, I. (2019) *The Master and His Emissary: The Divided Brain and the Making of the Western World.* New Haven: Yale University Press.

Sam Isaacson is a coach, coach supervisor and coaching technology thought leader.

PIPS Note-taking Model

Ingredients

None

Description

This tool is helpful for coaches in deciding what notes to capture from a session. Many coaches spend a significant amount of time writing during a session. This can be experienced by the client as if the coach is not listening or is more interested in capturing the information than understanding. PIPS (Personal, Ideas, Plans and Suggestions) are four headings under which the coach can capture a few thoughts, without feeling over-distracted by the need to capture everything the client says. It's also worth remembering that clients can ask to see your notes, so whatever you write, ensure you would be happy with the client reading these notes.

When does it work best?

The tool can be used in every coaching session and involves using a series of headings to capture the notes during the session which can provide a useful guide before the start of the next session with the client.

Step by step

1. The coach creates four headings in their note book:
   - Personal
   - Ideas
   - Plans
   - Suggestions.

   The aim is to captures notes under each heading, while avoiding capturing a linear story from the session.

2. Personal issues include non-sensitive, personal details. For example, if the client mentions the name of their partner, for example Sam. Or if their daughter, Florence, is playing in a netball tournament the following week. The notes may read: "Partner = Sam" or "Florence (daughter) network tournament".

3. The second heading is Ideas. These may be passing remarks that are worth capturing and may be worthy of exploration at a later time. For example, when focusing on one issue, a client may talk about the challenge of balancing work–home priorities. The notes may read: "Future topic? Balancing work–home priorities". Care should be taken not to offer a diagnosis or label the client's behaviour, thus avoiding phrases or terms such as 'depressed', 'bully' or 'victim'.

4. The third area for notes is Plans. At the end of a session note the client's plans of action. This is a good place to start the next session.

5. The fourth and final area is Suggestions. These may be comments, feedback or ideas from the client for the coach to action. There may have been a request for a book suggestion, website or other material to help the client explore their topic in more depth. The coach can action this after the session by sending an appropriate link or material to the client.

Jonathan Passmore is a chartered psychologist, accredited master coach, team coach, supervisor, author and professor at Henley Business School.

Missing Steps

Ingredients

A3 paper or flipchart

Post-it notes

Coloured pens

When does it work best?

This is a useful tool when used for action planning or at the stage of trying to explore the options that might be available. It is just as effective with individuals as with teams. It can help to generate ideas, breakdown complex situations or create a path to achieving a goal and to see past some roadblocks. It is also helpful in that it enables the client to play with the order in which things need to be done to achieve the goal.

Description

This is similar to the Story Boarding tool but helps clients start earlier in the process. It can be helpful in establishing what the goal is, before moving on to understanding what the steps to get there are. It also focusses on pulling out what skills and resources the client has available to them in pursuit of this goal.

Step by step

1. Using the large piece of paper, ask the client to draw the desired future outcome in the top-right-hand corner. They should be given as much time as possible to complete this task, to allow for free thought. Ask questions if required to assist the thinking process. You might also want to suggest that they draw this as a picture if the goal is initially hard for them to articulate.
2. Once this is complete, ask the client to explain it to you. Use this as an opportunity to explore the significance of what they have included.
3. Then ask the client to draw a step in the bottom-left corner. Ask them to list all their strengths and the resources available to them currently. Encourage them to come up with as many ideas as possible by asking, for example, "And what else?"
4. The objective now is to connect the bottom step with the desired future outcome. The client will be using Post-it notes for this. Therefore, ask your client to think of all the necessary steps to get between bottom-left and top-right and to complete as many Post-its as possible. Explain that these will be arranged later. The trick is to make sure enough steps are teased out and addressed as the way forward.
5. Ask them then to arrange these Post-it notes between the top-right and bottom-left step. The client can move these around as necessary as they arrange them.
6. Once the Post-it notes are in place, each step can be given a target date for completion. If necessary, Post-it notes can be amended or discarded as you go through this process together.

Maggie Grieve is an accredited leadership and team development coach, consultant and facilitator with 30 years of working with organisations and leaders across the world. She owns her own business, Ping Thinking, and is an external coach for NHS England.

Why Am I So Busy?

Ingredients

Pen and paper

Description

There is a certain pride clients can take in how busy they are, sometimes mistaking it for effectiveness. Keeping ourselves busy offers an excuse for us not to stop, think and consider priorities, longer-term goals and the impact we are actually making. Furthermore, a focus on dealing with transactional urgent tasks leaves us operating in a short-term bubble, failing to consider the bigger picture and longer-term goals. Such a realisation can come at any point in a career, when people burn out, question how far they have come against their early ambitions or consider the legacy they want to leave behind. This tool enables clients to increase their awareness about their business tendency, and as a result analyse their tasks, consider their relevance for business and career growth, and align their short-term priorities with long-term goals.

This tool combines a capacity-management model with solutions for wider delegation issues. A capacity management model provides insight into how successfully a client uses their resources (time, energy, money), adding the dimension of capability to the urgent/important prioritisation matrix; it recognises the impact a person's emotional and motivational states have on the prioritisation of tasks. The tool can also highlight reluctance to delegate.

Step by step

Phase 1: Analysis

The client is asked to consider both business needs and their own capabilities, reflecting what tasks they prioritise:

- Box A – High capability, high business need: Tasks that are enjoyable and fulfilling for them because they play to their strengths and capabilities, and are real business needs, and thus are appreciated by others. These tasks the client does very happily.
- Box B – High capability, low business need: Tasks that come naturally or easily to the client, often in their comfort zone, but which are of low importance to the business. The client often relapses into this comfort zone, avoiding engaging in more important tasks that are not playing to their current strengths.
- Box C – Low capability, low business need: Tasks that are not part of a client's core strengths and are also not important to the business. The client tends to avoid these tasks, so they are delayed and become a mental distraction from actual priorities.
- Box D – Low capability, high business need: Tasks that are high priority for the business but which the client doesn't feel confident or capable doing. These tasks the client avoids and deprioritises.

When does it work best?

This tool is particularly helpful when a client is facing burnout due to heavy workload and long working hours over an extended period of time, and is struggling to distinguish priorities in the volume of transactional tasks. It can also be helpful with clients who have issues prioritising in general or issues with delegating, perhaps having recently progressed from individual contributor to manager level.

B	A
Not important task	Important Task
Good at	Good at
C	**D**
Not important task	Important task
Not good at	Not good at

Analysing workload through the lens of these four boxes enables the client to understand why they are not tackling top business priorities, but also why they are focusing on tasks that have little value to their performance and career progression. As a result, it helps them gain clarity over the point of focus for their efforts.

Phase 2: Bigger picture, impact on career and growth

Ask the client:
- Which tasks have the greatest potential to add the most value to the business?
- Which tasks have the greatest potential to add the most value to their career and progression prospects?
- Which tasks will bring longer-term benefits?
- Which tasks will bring them the most visibility?
- Which tasks would make the biggest difference to their, and/or their team's, achievements and reputation?
- Which tasks will enable their team to grow?

Phase 3: Task sorting
- Ask the client to reflect on the tasks in Box B. Which of these could be delegated to others in their team (i.e. the client maintains final oversight, but doesn't get involved in the detail)? Which of these can the client train others to do? If needed, challenge the client to answer *why* they themselves must do this.
- Ask the client to reflect on the tasks in Box C. How can they disregard these and remove them from the list without feeling guilty? Whose approval might they need?
- Ask the client to reflect on the tasks in Box D. How can they develop the capabilities needed for successful execution of these tasks? What skills would they need? How can they develop them? Work with the client to create a development plan.

Work with the client to create an action plan based on the gained insights and decisions regarding each of the tasks. Repeat the exercise in three-to-six months to ensure the plan is achieved and that focus is in line with the business priorities and their career growth.

NB: It might happen that, while using the tool, it becomes obvious that the client has an issue with delegating. If so, discuss the need to tackle reluctance to delegate in the next session.

Reference

Lancer, N., Clutterback, D., and Megginson, D. (2016) *Techniques for Coaching and Mentoring* (2nd edition). London: Routledge.

Jelena Jovanovic Moon is a coach and psychologist, with degrees in coaching and organisational change and senior leadership roles in people management and organisational development.

The INSIGHT Cycle of Coaching and Mentoring

Ingredients

Picture of the INSIGHT Cycle

Pen and paper

Description

The INSIGHT coaching cycle gives a framework for coaching meetings and will help the client plan a way forward. The cycle and the acronym INSIGHT represent what happens within a coaching process, and the model is an excellent way to start working with individuals. The themes shown allow you to identify several vital interventions that must be well-thought-out at the contracting stage.

The INSIGHT model is relatively straightforward, and taking an inward-looking perspective and reflection is a good way of thinking about the model. The essence of good coaching using this model is that the development process is two-way and depends on the two parties having absolute trust in each other.

INSIGHT is an acronym derived from the first letter of each of the seven coaching process stages. There is no time limit mentioned in the cycle, so it can be adjusted to meet the needs of each individual or organisation. The visual aspect of the diagram gives a memorable picture of the whole process, and clients can see what they can expect to explore at each stage.

The method was developed by Eileen Hutchinson as part of a research programme for Hertfordshire University on peer-to-peer coaching and

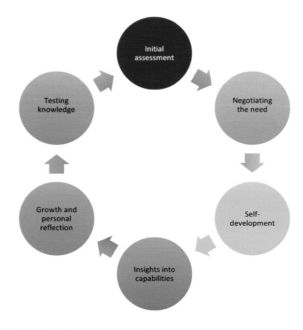

Diagram: The INSIGHT Cycle

mentoring (Hale and Hutchinson, 2012). The detail of each stage is emergent and the coaching journey remains broadly the same. It is predominantly used during the contracting stage and for check-ins where appropriate, such as inter-personal development, contract management and pastoral care for executive coaches in corporate organisations.

The cycle is a question-driven activity, providing a way to develop meaningful conversations that fully support all stakeholders to engage in the coaching plan and it is designed to help coaches deliver a complete coaching cycle.

When does it work best?

The technique works best when an organisation or individual needs to see how the coaching process will be designed. It outlines how to manage the coaching intervention within an organisational context and supports coaches and client to reflect on an ongoing basis (e.g. continuing coaching, mid-way review, evaluating, concluding, etc.). It offers a flexible method enabling the coach to include various tools and techniques. Each stage of the cycle begins with a conversation about how that particular phase will work and in what will support both client and coach to engage in the session. The testing stage will give the individual time to experiment with new skills and knowledge while gaining a deeper appreciation for their personal and professional achievements.

At the core of the process is a set of questions: **"What are the main things you learned from the sessions? How do you intend to apply the learning? How will you measure the effectiveness of this?"** These questions afford the individual the opportunity to reflect, review and realise the impact and outcomes of their actions. Each stage asks the coach to explore how the process works, how they think about the sessions, how the individual becomes self-aware, the impact of the tools and techniques, and the importance of the coaching relationship. The development testing stage will allow the individual to complete the programme or initiate additional sessions. This is where the client can start to put in place a reflective way of thinking and discuss what has worked well for them or what they need to add or change; they could decide on a new approach, goal or goals, initiating a new coaching plan.

Step by step

1. **I – Initial assessment –** The initial assessment will give the coach the opportunity to build rapport with the client whilst eliciting the core requirements for the coaching intervention.
2. **N – Negotiating the coaching plan –** Negotiating the coaching plan is a key component of the INSIGHT Cycle, covering environment, ethical practice, preparation, time commitment and paperwork.

3. **S – Self-development and new behaviours –** The self-development plan or CPD (continuous personal development) will enable the client to identify areas for development. It will afford the coach the opportunity to suggest and discuss new behaviour techniques or new learning with the purpose of bringing about personal change.

4. **I – Insight into own capabilities –** Once the client engages in the first part of the INSIGHT Cycle they will identify and discover insights into their own capabilities, including reviewing both their strengths and weaknesses, allowing for a deeper understanding of their personal beliefs, values and goals.

5. **G – Growth and personal reflection –** The growth and personal reflection period will give the client the time to reflect on the interventions provided, with a view to monitor, review and evaluate what has worked well and what may need to be modified.

6. **H – Hierarchy of needs –** This element of the cycle will give both parties insight into motivation and achievements to date, ensuring the basic needs of the coaching intervention have been completed before moving on to discussing more complex needs.

7. **T – Testing new skills and knowledge –** The testing stage will give the client time to test their new skills and knowledge (within their work and lives), while gaining a deeper appreciation for their personal and professional achievements.

8. **Review the process with the following questions of yourself as client:**
Am I asking insightful questions?
Am I getting honest answers to these questions?

Reference

Hale, R., and Hutchinson, E. (2012) *Understanding Coaching and Mentoring.* MX Publishing.

Eileen Hutchinson is an executive accredited coach and career counsellor, and has authored a series of coaching books.

IMPROVE

Ingredients

None

When does it work best?

The IMPROVE framework is a useful tool to share with clients who experience high levels of stress or rapidly changing, and thus uncontrollable, emotions. By focusing on relaxation techniques, the client can draw upon the technique that works best for them in a specific situation, or use a range of such techniques to better manage the stressful situation they are facing across a working week or month.

Description

IMPROVE can be a useful framework for supporting clients to engage in relaxation techniques. The framework is drawn from dialectic behavioural therapy (DBT), a counselling approach initially developed for clients with strong emotional urges. These may result, for example, from high levels of stress. The IMPROVE framework can help clients remember that they have a wealth of different tools they can call upon to manage these high-stress situations. By using one of the relaxation or emotional management techniques they may be able to better manage these high-stress periods or situations.

IMPROVE stands for:

- **Imagery**: Imagine how an event ends successfully, or imagine a peaceful, relaxing scene.
- **Meaning**: Relate a positive purpose or meaning to the emotion being felt.
- **Prayer**: Use prayer, or if you are not religious, repeat a personal mantra, such as "This will pass".
- **Relaxation**: Engage in a relaxation or meditation techniques, such as focusing on slow breathing.
- **One thing** at a time: Keep your attention and focus on the present moment using mindfulness.
- **Vacation**: Take a short break, such as taking a brief walk or reading a novel for 10 minutes.
- **Encouragement**: Be a cheerleader for yourself and remind yourself that you can do it!

Step by step

1. Share the IMPROVE framework with the client.
2. Invite them to consider different examples that might work for them in each category and to write these down, as part of developing their personal stress-management toolkit.
3. Invite them to consider which tools they are initially drawn to.
4. Invite the client to try out each of the techniques over the coming week or month, before the next session, and keep a log of their experience: When did they use it? How did they find it helped?
5. Review the client's log in the following session. Encourage the client to keep the framework as a toolkit and to use the tools which work best for them when stressful situations arise.

Jonathan Passmore is a chartered psychologist, accredited master coach, team coach, supervisor, author and professor at Henley Business School.

Reference

McKay, M., Wood, J.C., and Brantley, J. (2019) *The Dialectical Behavior Therapy Skills Workbook: Practical DBT Exercises for Learning Mindfulness, Interpersonal Emotional Regulation and Distress Tolerance*. Oakland: New Harbinger.

Re-engaging as a Recovering Leader

Ingredients

A2/A3/A4 paper sheets

Pencils/pens

Description

This is a process of specific powerful questions to create an on ramp back into leadership after a recovery break for clients who lead within their organisations. After a life-changing event like grappling with addiction, a serious, even life-threatening, health challenge, a mental breakdown or other psychological blow, people are usually changed forever. To coach people in recovery and back to wellness is to travel with them to a new land where their life is not what it was. When these people are also holding leadership roles in their lives, the way they lead is going to change. It *ought* to change, for it is impossible to return to who you were before such a life event. There will be challenges to this shift in leadership. Values often change too. What seemed very important before the challenge is less so afterwards. When a client returns to a leadership environment, the people they lead are often unsure what to expect. Are they getting the same leader back again? Will they be better, worse? How are they to be treated? Are they still to be respected?

The client is best served by meeting these questions head on and preparing themselves so that who they have become, or are becoming, is clear to them – and likewise how they plan to lead their team after their life-changing experiences. Where you start with a client depends on your relationship with them. They may be new clients or they may be existing ones who you have coached for a while. You may need to get to know their leadership styles and behaviours, or you may have a good grasp of them already. Either way, this approach can provide great benefit for the client's awareness of their changing leadership.

When does it work best?

The more consideration a client can give to the issue of re-engaging as a leader after a break the better. Ideally you can enter into this process before they return to their role. Sometimes time and organisational demands can mean that it all happens too quickly. In that scenario, clients may well come with some concerns and anxiety about how their leadership is going to play out going forwards. It is good to be mindful that issues of personal authority and redefining leadership might trigger past events that the client feels uncomfortable about, even some shame and other hard-to-cope-with emotions.

Step by step

The process can be divided into the following headings that provide powerful questions for the/a client.

Re-engaging as a Recovering Leader

1. Ask: "Who were you as a leader before you had this life-changing experience of [insert what they have been going through here – for example, depression, illness, addiction or trauma]"?
    Coach them to become clear on who they were before the life event derailed or interfered with their life. Note that they may speak in the present tense – for example, "As a leader I am…" – and that is fine. Do not correct them but coach them to fully explore this question. Ask them to make notes as they go if they wish. Once they have made this exploration, ask them these following further questions (you obviously can improvise on these as the moment requires).

2. Ask appropriate questions such as: "In what ways have you been changed by your experience?" and "What do you now know or believe about your role a leader as a result of what has happened to you? What are your insights?" Again, coach them in exploring these questions, paying attention to which of their values have been reduced in importance and which amplified. Listen too for any description of behaviours that they link to these shifts in values. For example, they may say that they realise that they were spending too much time at work and demanding that their teams did too. They may now want to shift that balance between work and outside-work life, spending more time with loved ones or pursuing other activities. Be sure that you or the client capture the way that they have changed.

3. Once you have explored this with them it is useful to bring a specific focus on the core significant elements of change that have taken place. This is usefully done on large sheets of paper where you describe who they were as a leader (PAST) and then another with who they are now as a leader (PRESENT).

4. Explore with your client how they might communicate these changes with their team at work. There are a number of ways this can be done and it is best that the client themselves design the method. It is important to emphasise that they can communicate to their team along the same lines that you have explored with them. This could involve addressing their team on the following:
    *   "How I was leading you and what was driving that" (how I used to behave and why)
    *   "What I have learned from my experience" (what happened to me and what I have learned)
    *   "How that has changed how I will lead" (what I am going to do now and how it will be different)
    *   "What you can expect specifically" (what has changed about what I will ask and what I will ask of you)
    *   "What do you need to know?" This provides the opportunity for people in the team to ask questions and for clarification.
    Sometimes at this point, when the client is imagining themselves talking at work, they can find it hard to know how to speak to their team or employees.

5. Spend some time rehearsing with them how they can find the words that will fit best and go through it until they are confident. Role play can be very helpful. Another option that can be added is to ask the client, as a piece of homework, to write a letter to their team that sets out this information. This letter is not going to be sent but you can work with them to explore the process through the letter.

6. Finally, most leaders have one or two very simple but profound ways of defining how they see themselves as a leader. These can be expressed in simple statements including, for example:
    *   "As a leader I am powerful and honest"
    *   "As a leader I am focussed and unyielding"
    *   "As a leader I am humble and open."

    Propose to your client that it can be useful to craft a statement on a before-and-after basis with your client. Explain that this allows them the opportunity to shift the core essence of their leadership energy as a result of their life experience. So they might go from "As a leader I was self-focussed, pushy and ambitious" to "As a leader I am compassionate, balanced and clear".

    Explain that this process cannot be done thoroughly in a quick session; it is best worked at over a few sessions. It can be mixed in with other topics in the client's life that will naturally lead to the topic of leadership and who they are.

7. Revisit this process over ongoing coaching sessions. Should a new personal statement emerge from the sessions, encourage it to be used as an anchor on which to focus their future leadership.

Anthony Eldridge-Rogers is a coach, facilitator, author and speaker specialising in Recovery and Wellness Coaching and the Meaning Centred Coaching model he created.

4+1 Questions

Ingredients

Paper and pen

The 4+1 template as A4 document (optional)

Flipchart paper and pens, if using with a group

When does it work best?

4+1 questions can be used one to one or with groups to help the client step back and reflect on progress, view a challenge from different perspectives or, for groups, to build consensus around a way forward. It can be used periodically as part of a continuous improvement and learning cycle.

Description

4+1 Questions is a simple tool for reflective practice that can be used to help people review their progress in relation to a task or challenge and to plan next steps. The questions take the client through a process that is aligned with the What? So What? Now What? framework for reflective practice described by Rolfe and colleagues (2001). The questions are intended to be answered by more than one person, to ensure a range of different perspectives inform the way forward.

4+1 Questions was originally designed to support person-centred practice in UK social care by Helen Sanderson but is widely applicable to coaching. It invites a conversation around four main questions:

- What have you tried?
- What have you learned?
- What are you pleased about?
- What are you concerned about?

The answers to these questions lead to the 'plus one' question:

- Based on what we know, what should we do next?

The questions can be adapted to suit the client or situation. For example, you could ask:

- What's working? What's not working? What is possible? What is useful? What next?

Or:

- What do you want to Keep/Improve/Start/Stop (KISS) and what next?

The tool's power is in the neatness of the four questions, which enable a deeper level of reflection than might be possible by only asking: how do you think it's going?

Step by step

1. Introduce the template – you can print it out or draw it. If using with a group, draw the template on sheets of flipchart paper and stick it around the room. If working online, you can facilitate this using an online whiteboard such as Jamboard.

4+1 Questions

Diagram: 4+1 questions

What have we tried?	What have we learned?
What are we pleased about?	What are we concerned about?

What do we do next?

2. In a one-to-one situation – use the template to open up the client's reflection based around each of the four questions. Use probing questions to draw out clarity, detail and deeper reflection. For example, "What else have you learned?", "What else?", "What more could you say about that?" or "How do you know that?" and "Tell me more about that".

3. Invite reflection from different perspectives by asking questions such as "What would others say about that?", "What's another way of viewing that?", "What would your manager/direct report/customer/competitor think/do/feel about that?" or "What perspective haven't you mentioned yet?"

4. If using with a group, depending on the size of the group you can either get individuals to fill in their own large template, or get people to work in pairs or small groups, then invite them to walk around to see what others have written. Participants can add detail or comments on Post-its. You can help the group gauge consensus by inviting people to vote for the top three things they think are most important using sticky dots.

5. Ensure you build in enough time for reflection and working out next steps through the '+1' question.

References

Rolfe, G., et al. (2001) *Critical Reflection in Nursing and the Helping Professions: A User's Guide.* Palgrave Macmillan: Basingstoke.

Sanderson, H. (n.d.) 4+1 Questions Template. Available from: http://helensandersonassociates.co.uk/person-centred-practice/person-centred-thinking-tools/4-plus-1-questions [Retrieved 25 April 2023].

Catherine Wilton is a coach, supervisor and leadership development specialist with over 20 years' experience of supporting individuals and groups. She is Director of the NHS Leadership for Personalised Care programme and Collaborative Leadership Academy.

Friendly Advice

Ingredients

None

When does it work best?

This can be impactful when a client is finding it difficult to generate or decide between options, and also when there is a lot of negative self-talk.

Description

Friendly Advice is a really simple exercise that can be surprisingly effective. It consists of the client imagining themselves in two possible scenarios: 1. A person trusted by the client explains their view of an issue to the client. 2. The client imagines what they would advise a trusted person to do if they were in the same situation. In this way, the change of perspective may free the client from some of the constraints that have held them back.

Step by step

1. Once the reality has been fully explored and the options are being considered, ask the client to imagine someone they really care about (friend, relative, colleague, etc.). Once that person is in their minds, set the scene with this person. Where would they meet? What are they doing? Once this is defined, ask the client one or both of the following questions:
   a. What would they say to this person if they came for advice? This exercise can be repeated with more than one person. If so, they can also see if there are any differences.
   b. What advice would a person they trust/admire give them? This exercise can be repeated with more than one person. If so, they can also see if there are any differences.
2. Carry on exploring the answers and how they might pursue their options, given this advice.
3. Continue the session as you normally would.

Claudia Day is a coach and entrepreneur, co-founder of My Coaching Place, part of the AC UK leadership team, and holds a master's in coaching and behavioural change (Henley) and a master's in business administration (MIT).

Tetralemma

Ingredients

Enough space for the client to move within the room

Five pieces of A4 paper and a marker

When does it work best?

When the coach feels that their client is stuck in a dilemma, then Tetralemma provides a very useful process to widen the client's perspective and allow them to take more information into account before making the final decision. Tetralemma works best when it is done in an embodied way, using 'floor markers'.

Description

When we are in a dilemma, typically we are thinking about two options that we need to choose from – for example, whether you continue working in the current company (Option1) or quit to start your own business as a coach (Option 2). When we are in dilemma, the energy is blocked between the two options and the perspective gets narrowed. One way to approach a dilemma is to do a pros-and-cons analysis of each option and take a 'rational decision' based on its results. Although such an approach might look efficient and useful for some issues of smaller significance, when confronted with more important life issues like changing a job, moving to another country or selling your company, it would be wiser to take into account a broader field of information, using various ways of knowing, including rational mind, intuition, emotional reasoning and whole-body sensing.

Tetralemma is based on Buddhist tradition and was originally used by judges in India. It has been 'rediscovered' in the field of systemic coaching and constellations by Insa Sparrer and Matthias Varga von Kibed. In essence, contrary to the common Western type of thinking, each dilemma has at least four options to consider, hence the name Tetralemma:

- Option A
- Option B
- Both A and B
- Neither A nor B.

In addition to these four, there is also an additional fifth option, that asks the client to think even more freely, beyond the frame of the current thinking:

- None of these and beyond this all.

Step by step

1. Start with the two options in the original dilemma. Write them down (or ask the client to do it) on two pieces of paper. For example:
    Option A: Continue working in the current company
    Option B: Start working as a coach.

These papers will be used as floor markers. Now ask the client to position the two papers on the floor opposing each other at a certain distance (depending on the room, make sure that the two papers are at least two metres from each other).

Tetralemma

When the client is ready, ask them to step onto one of the two options, to stand on the paper and fully connect in an embodied way with that option. You might like to ask the client the following:

- How does it feel to be there?
- How do you feel it in your body?
- How is the energy in that place?
- What does it look like to be here?
- What do you gain here? And what do you lose?
- What does this place bring to you?
- Who is serving whom here?
- What are the opportunities you have there?

After exploring the first option, ask the client to step onto the paper with the other option and again explore the second option, asking similar exploration questions.

2. When this is done, ask the client *slowly and mindfully* to move from one option to the other and back, sensing the change that this movement brings to the client's body. Ask them to share any insights that arise.
3. After this walk is done, invite the client to write another two papers:

'Both A and B' or simply 'Both'

'Neither A nor B' or simply 'Neither'.

These two papers should be placed so as to form another 'axis' on the floor (see diagram).

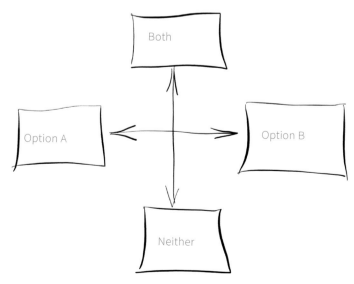

Tetralemma

4. First, ask the client to step onto 'Both' and explore it with the following questions:
   - How does it feel here?
   - How does it feel in your body?
   - What comes to your mind about what this place might be?
   - What does/might this 'both' look like?
   - What are the new opportunities that you can have from here?
   - What becomes possible here?
   - What does it bring that's new?
5. Then invite the client to take the fourth position, 'Neither A nor B', and explore it with similar questions to those of the previous step.
6. After exploring this position, take the client out of the map (in the 'meta position') and tell them that there is one more additional position which is called 'None of these and beyond this all' that might represent something completely different that is also important to take into account when making this decision (note: it is not about providing an escape!). It might also have a quality of 'what life wants from you'.

Write that fifth floor marker and invite the client to place it outside the square created by the four previous options.

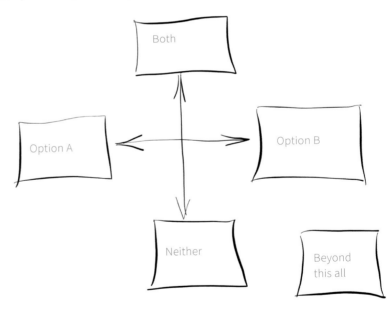

Invite the client to step in there, take a deep breath, tune in and feel what this place might be. Anything that comes from that place is welcome. Very often this place evokes either some longer-term personal vision of the client or a passion to be taken into account when making the final decision.

7. After completing the exploration, invite the client to take a final walk through the field and harvest everything that is important for the

Tetralemma

decision. The final walk happens in the same order: starting from Option A, moving to Option B, then to 'Both', then to 'Neither' and finally to 'Beyond this all'.

8. Finally, sit down with the client, harvest the insights and continue with more classic coaching questions towards the planning of the next steps.

Reference

Sparrer, I. (2007) *Miracle, Solutions and System*. London: Solutions Books.

Darko Markovic is a systemic coach supporting organisations and leaders in making systemic changes and overcoming blocking patterns.

A Model for GOODBYES

Ingredients

None

When does it work best?

The GOODBYES model works best when coaches and clients approach the end of their coaching relationship, particularly when complex emotions or unresolved issues are present. This approach is well-suited for coaches who prioritise ethical practice, focus on client-centred outcomes, and appreciate the importance of continuous professional development and learning from their experiences. The model can serve as a reflective tool before the last session and as a structure to navigate the final session itself.

Description

The GOODBYES model is a structured, reflective process designed to help executive coaches and their clients manage the ending phase of a coaching relationship in partnership. Grounded in research, the model enables both the coach and the client to navigate the emotional, ethical and practical challenges of ending their relationship, fostering a sense of closure and growth, and a smooth transition. It aims to address the ending process's emotional and practical aspects.

Step by step

G – Gratitude: Begin the final session by expressing gratitude for the shared experiences, insights and progress made during the coaching partnership. This can foster a positive atmosphere and encourage clients to reflect on their growth and accomplishments. It also allows a space for reciprocation without obligation.

- "In reflecting on our coaching relationship, which aspects have been particularly valuable or meaningful to you?"
- "How have we, working together, contributed to your personal and professional growth?"
- "How can you recognise and appreciate your commitment and progress?"

O – Objectives: Together, revisit the objectives established at the beginning of the coaching partnership and collaboratively assess the progress made towards achieving them. This can help the client recognise their accomplishments and understand their journey.

- "What were the initial objectives of our coaching relationship?"
- "Which objectives have you achieved and which ones require further attention?"
- "How has working towards these objectives impacted your personal and professional life?"

O – Opportunities: Explore, with the client, the new opportunities that have emerged as a result of the coaching partnership. Encourage the client to envision their growth and development beyond the coaching relationship.

- "What opportunities have emerged from your coaching journey?"
- "How can you leverage these opportunities for continued growth and development?"
- "What potential future engagements or support networks can help you sustain your progress?"

D – Decisions: Facilitate a conversation around the decisions the client has made or will need to make due to the coaching partnership. Support the client in recognising their agency and ownership of their progress.

- "What key decisions will you need to make to continue your progress in the future?"
- "How can you apply the insights and learnings from the coaching process to inform these decisions?"
- "What support or resources might you need to make these decisions confidently and effectively?"

B – Barriers: Discuss any remaining barriers or challenges the client may face in achieving their objectives and collaboratively brainstorm ways to overcome them. Empower the client to feel supported and equipped to tackle future challenges.

- "What potential barriers or challenges might you encounter as you continue your personal and professional journey?"
- "How can you apply the strategies and learnings from the coaching process to overcome these future barriers?"
- "What additional resources or support networks can help you address these challenges and ensure your ongoing success?"

Y – Yearning: Create a space for the client to reflect on any yearnings or unmet needs that may remain at the end of the coaching partnership. Together, explore how such feelings can be addressed in future coaching relationships or other personal or professional contexts.

- "What unmet needs or desires have surfaced during our coaching relationship?"
- "How can you address these yearnings in future relationships or other contexts?"
- "What emotions do you associate with these unmet needs or desires, and how can you process them?"

E – Ending: Encourage the client to reflect on the coaching partnership as a whole and the process of concluding the relationship. Share final thoughts or feelings about the coaching journey and explore strategies to maintain the progress made. This can help the client experience a sense of closure and satisfaction with the coaching partnership.

- "How can we create a sense of closure and accomplishment in our final coaching session?"
- "What practices might help you recognise and honour the conclusion of our coaching relationship?"
- "How can you ensure a smooth transition from the coaching relationship to the next stage of your personal and professional journey?"

S – Safety: Close by committing to honour confidentiality after the coaching relationship ends. Reinforce the duty to keep the client's information secure and continue upholding ethical standards, ensuring a sense of trust and safety even after the conclusion of the coaching journey.

- "Are there any specific agreements we need to establish to ensure ongoing confidentiality and safety in relation to the topics we've discussed?"

Derek Hill is a leadership and behavioural coach, specialising in transitions, be they beginnings, belongings or endings. He is also the founder of hi-5 Coaching.

Motivate–demotivate Grid (MDG)

Ingredients

Pen and paper

Flipchart/Digital Whiteboard

Description

Understanding what motivates us is an important aspect of our own development, but rarely do others ask us what motivates us or, equally, what can act as a source of demotivation. This exercise, which can be used in team coaching, provides a way for individuals to share their motivations and the factors that act to demotivate them at work, and specifically in their communications with fellow team members. Individuals complete by themselves a simple four-box grid and then share this with colleagues in a process facilitated by the team coach.

I work well when…	If you want to motivate me…
Work is harder when…	If you want to demotivate me…

Step by step

1. Using a digital whiteboard (or a real-world flipchart) write out the four-box grid.
2. Explain the framework to the team and how understanding ourselves and others in the team will contribute to enhanced team performance.
3. Invite team members to spend time producing three-to-five examples for each box, working quietly and independently.
4. Invite the team members, one by one, to write their thoughts on the digital whiteboard and explain each in turn to their colleagues in the team. (This should be done without naming other colleagues or referring to specific situations.)
5. The team members should listen and avoid interrupting.
6. At the end of each input, the team coach may ask for clarification before inviting the next person to share their input.
7. Finally, each team member is invited to reflect and then to share their insights from the exercise individually, with the team coach managing the process.

Jonathan Passmore is a chartered psychologist, accredited master coach, team coach, supervisor, author and professor at Henley Business School.

Job Crafting

Ingredients

Pen(s)

Paper

Whiteboard or
flipchart

When does it work best?

Introducing this
concept works
best when a client
feels or has little
autonomy or
control within their
jobs, and their
ability to influence
change is limited. It
can also be
particularly useful
when clients need
to establish more
vitality at work.

Reference

Slemp, G. (2017) Job
Crafting. In L.G. Oades,
M.F. Steger, A.D. Fave and
J. Passmore (eds), *The
Wiley Blackwell Handbook
of The Psychological
Strengths-Based
Approaches at Work*.
Oxford: Wiley Blackwell,
pp.342–365.

Description

The concept of job crafting is based upon potential physical or cognitive changes people can make in tasks or relational boundaries of their work. Through modifying aspects of jobs, people can improve the fit between their own needs, abilities and preferences, and the characteristics of their jobs. People can do this through the following different strategies:

Task crafting (doing): Changing the scope of their sphere of action, for example, doing different tasks at work that acquire new skills or ensuring that their strengths and talents are used.

Relational crafting (connections): Changing relationships at work by modifying the nature or extent of interactions – for example, increasing contact with colleagues they find inspiring or aligning work with their preferences for sociability.

Cognitive crafting (thinking): Using cognitive strategies by changing the way in which they think about and perceive job tasks – for example, reframing mundane tasks as more important tasks or using refocusing or recalibrating techniques to initiate changes in their thinking.

Step by step

1. Invite the client to describe a typical day at work.
2. As you are listening to the client, notice what they are describing in terms of what they do, the connections they have and what they are thinking.
3. Introduce the concept of job crafting and the three different strategies available.
4. Invite the client to start to explore one or each of the strategy areas. (This will depend on what you noticed from the description of the typical day or week at work.)
5. Ask probing questions to evoke in the client any changes that they feel they could make to gain more control over their work. You may like to share with them what you noticed as they described their typical day.
6. Then ask the client to share what a work day would look like after they made any of the changes.
7. Ask the client to reflect on what felt different between the two days that were described in steps 1 and 6.
8. Encourage the client to explore how they will bring any changes to life when they are next working and what support they need to make these changes.

Deb McEwen is an experienced accredited coach who has held senior leadership roles (NZ, AU and UK) and has an extensive background in health and wellbeing.

Selective Realism

Ingredients

Selective Realism scale

Paper and pen

When does it work best?

This tool is most effective in the middle of the coaching sessions when the client is considering making a change, and at the end of coaching sessions when coaching outcomes may have been achieved.

Description

The Selective Realism conceptual model (Shams, 2022) is based on the notion that individuals are active environmental agents capable of interpreting and reflecting on present life experiences. The emergence of Selective Realism during coaching sessions provides individuals with a mental map promoting personal agency for self-growth. Selective Realism helps individuals to understand and interpret their lived experience, and to reflect on their thoughts, feelings and actions to bring changes to their lives. The individual is thus able to guide their own development using the coaching process to reflect on and plan their future actions.

Step by step

1. Invite the client to reflect on their coaching experiences to date and whether they can identify any changes in their understanding of their present life experiences.
2. Invite your client to keep focusing on the changes they have noted as a result of their coaching and what they will do to make this change sustainable.
3. Ask your client to rate the changes in their thinking and new ways of understanding their immediate experiences on a five-point Likert scale of 0–5, where 0 = none and 5 = most.
4. The lowest score denotes no change in the cognitive and behavioural functions of a client and the highest score denotes complete change in these domains, implying effective coaching intervention for making a change.

Reference

Shams, M. (2022) *Psychology in Coaching Practice*. England: McGraw-Hill and OU Press.

Dr Manfusa Shams is a chartered psychologist, coach, mentor, author and supervisor.

Alternative Perspectives

Ingredients

None

When does it work best?

This interactive and thought-provoking exercise is helpful for clients who would like to gain greater insight into others' perspectives on a complex situation, or who would like to challenge their assumptions and thinking. It works well with clients who enjoy working experientially and in situations where there may be many different (and potentially competing) stake-holder needs and viewpoints.

Julie Flower is a leadership development coach, consultant and facilitator, with a specialism in improvi-sation in complex systems. She is also an external tutor in executive coaching at Henley Business School.

Description

Alternative Perspectives is a systemic approach for individuals or teams in which people are asked to imagine inhabiting the role or position of others within their system, to gain greater insight, empathy and awareness. Clients select people, organisations or even objects or other entities within their system and write down and share open questions that they would like to ask themselves from that systemic perspective.

Step by step

1. Ask the client (or clients, if a team) to identify a number of stakeholders or entities within their system, who are relevant to the coaching theme. It may help for the client to map out the key elements of the system in some way, such as with objects or by drawing.
2. The type of people or entities will vary depending on the situation but it is important to encourage your client to think widely, considering a range of perspectives, and all those who might be able to influence, or be affected by, any change.
3. If working in a group, allocate a perspective to each individual – for example, "Ali will be a local GP, Jane will be the executive team of the local hospital and Dennis will be a resident living with diabetes". Working with up to six perspectives is usually manageable.
4. In turn, invite each person to ask a question from their perspective. If working with an individual client, invite them to consider each perspective in turn. Encourage the use of open, thought-provoking questions, which are informed by what the clients imagine might be the concerns or viewpoints of different stakeholders.
5. At this point, the individual or team may wish to respond immediately with their thoughts or take the questions away for further reflection.
6. Encourage insight by asking the individual or team to reflect on what has changed for them or what insight they have gained through the exercise, and what they would like to do next.
7. Of course, the questions are not coming from 'real' people or entities within the system, but the process of generating and responding to questions usually provides great insight and awareness for clients, opening up new potential perspectives or wider considerations.

TIPP

Ingredients

None

When does it work best?

Like other DBT approaches, the tool works best for clients with strong emotional urges and who feel overwhelmed by these emotions. It can also work well for clients experiencing high levels of stress. The tool is best used as part of a wider DBT approach.

Description

TIPP is a tool derived from dialectical behavioural therapy (DBT), which was originally developed to support clients with borderline personality disorder (Lineham, 1993) and has subsequently been used to support clients who experience strong emotional urges and high levels of stress. This technique can help clients who experience overwhelming emotions and who find it difficult to think clearly during these episodes. Like many DBT approaches, TIPP is an acronym. It stands for:

1. **Temperature**: Raised body temperature is often a feature of raised heart rate. We can decrease our heart rate by lowering our body temperature, such as by splashing our face with cold water or stepping out if the weather is below 12 degrees. If our mood needs to be raised, a hot bath or shower can have a positive effect to raise our heart rate and our mood.
2. **Intense exercise**: Being overwhelmed emotionally can build up a surge of energy. Intense exercise can be a really good way to dissipate this. You could go for a long run, get out a skipping rope or chop logs, for example.
3. **Paced breathing**.
4. **Progressive muscle relaxation**.

Step by step

1. Share the model with the client and explain the benefits of the four steps of TIPP (temperature reduction, intense exercise, paced breathing and progressive muscle relaxation).
2. Explore temperature with the client. Depending on the challenge faced by the client, invite them to consider ways that suit them of raising or lowering their body temperature and thus managing the emotional challenge they face. For example, this might include stepping away during a heated conversation for a comfort break, and using the opportunity to splash cold water on their face; or in colder climates, stepping outside without a coat to reduce body temperature.
3. Explore intense exercise with the client. What could the client do to undertake more active exercise? For example, could the client undertake a short, fast-paced run for 20 minutes at lunchtime or the end of the day, or engage in a high-intensity exercise class? Another option might be for the client to keep a skipping rope in their office to engage in five minutes of skipping until they are out of breath. In offering this, it may also be wise to check whether clients have any health conditions and invite them to seek medical advice first.

4. Explore paced breathing with the client. This involves breathing in through the nose (abdominal breathing), holding the breath for six seconds and then breathing out through the mouth, slowly and in a controlled way, completely emptying the lungs.

5. Explore progressive muscle relaxation with the client. This is best done from a seated position. Invite the client to start from the top of their body. They should first become aware of this part of their body and then start deliberately tensing this area, holding the tension for a few seconds. This should be followed by gradually relaxing the part of the body and imagining breathing into the area. The client can then be invited to gradually work through each part of their body, down to their toes, following the same process. The process may take one-to-two minutes as the client deliberately and slowly works through each part of their body, tensing, releasing and breathing into each to relax.

Reference

Lineham, M.M. (1993) *Cognitive Behavioural Treatment for Borderline Personality Disorder*. New York: Guildford Press.

Jonathan Passmore is a chartered psychologist, accredited master coach, team coach, supervisor, author and professor at Henley Business School.

Tannenbaum and Schmidt's Continuum

Ingredients

A drawing of Tannenbaum and Schmidt's leadership model (available online)

When does it work best?

The model can be helpful for clients reflecting on their leadership style, goal-setting, empowerment, delegation or decision-making. It can be particularly useful with inexperienced managers who may be working with experienced teams that are seeking more empowerment. It is also very helpful in helping clients to adopt a flexible or situational leadership style.

Description

This tool is a leadership and management model that helps a client reflect on and understand their leadership style and decision-making. Tannenbaum and Schmidt's leadership model identifies seven stages along a continuum with 'Use of authority by manager' at one end and 'Area of freedom for subordinates' at the other. At the far left of the continuum, the leader or manager sets goals, makes decisions and directs action. At the far-right end of the continuum, the leader allows the group to share decision-making and goal-setting activities. Moving along the continuum from left to right, a leader or manager gradually gives up solo decision-making power, progressively involving the group or team until it effectively becomes self-managing.

Step by step

1. Introduce the model to a client as being helpful when reflecting on leadership style, empowerment, decision-making and so forth.
2. Help the client to identify where they tend to operate on the continuum and whether they always adopt the same position or whether that depends on the context.
3. The coach may ask questions such as "With your current team, where on the continuum do you usually tend to feel comfortable?", "What would help you to change position?" or "How might your team react if you adopted a different position on the continuum?"
4. Allow the client to reflect on their situation and explore possibilities for moving forward.

Reference

Tannenbaum, R., and Schmidt, W.H. (1973) How to Choose a Leadership Pattern. *Harvard Business Review*. Available from: https://hbr.org/1973/05/how-to-choose-a-leadership-pattern [Retrieved 1 May 2023].

Dave Crome is an accredited coach, consultant and Action-Centred Leadership trainer.

Lands Work

Ingredients

Flipchart paper and pens

Space to move around

Description

Lands Work is an Organisation and Relationship Systems Coaching tool that can be used to help increase empathy and broaden the perspectives of team members.

There are three key metaphors in Lands Work:

1. The *well-behaved tourist* – those who visit come with appreciation for the new land, free from judgement. They show curiosity and are open to learning.
2. The *generous and kind host* – those who welcome others into their land are honoured to show visitors around and to showcase what they are proud of, or what is important to them as locals. Hosts are patient and open in answering visitors' questions and provide clarity.
3. The notion of *simply visiting* – when entering a new land, baggage is left at the door. Those visiting are supported by the idea that they can return to their own land at any time to ground themselves.

As well as visiting the lands of colleagues, there is the opportunity to co-create a new shared land – *Our Land* – a space that everyone feels they can support and occupy. Our Land typically results in a shared 'charter' (behavioural conditions and values for success).

When does it work best?

Lands Work is useful for teams where functional identities are strong and where there is a need to create a new 'land' for the collective, so the team can occupy a space where it is more than the sum of its parts.

The tool works particularly well where leaders are entrenched or stuck in their position or perspective, as it focuses on developing empathy and understanding. It enables teams to appreciate difference and find ways to proactively create from these differences rather than defaulting to "Why don't you do things my way?" or "Why can't you be more like me?" type thinking.

By moving around the room, it makes use of spatial reorientation, particularly as the team move from their own lands to co-create their collective new land.

Clients comment that they find it engaging, energising and memorable – we find that teams refer back to it over the course of a team coaching engagement and incorporate it into their language, using it to call out when they readopted their functional hats – for example, "I think we have reverted to our individual lands – how can we reframe this to tackle it from our combined land?"

Step by step

1. **Exploring each person's lands**
- Invite leaders to take a piece of flipchart paper and write the name of their land on it. They can then place it on the floor around the edge of the room and stand on their own land.
- Ensure everyone knows they need to pay attention as each person shares about their land, as they will be asked to play back what they have heard later on.
- In turn, invite each leader to speak from their land and answer the following:
  o What do you love about your land?
  o What is difficult in your land?
  o What else do you want others to know about your land?

2. **Visiting each other's lands**
- Now invite leaders to visit each of the lands. For example, the CFO steps back from their land and everyone else visits by moving on (near to) the CFO's flipchart on the floor. Ask the visitors to explain what they know about the land based on what they have heard in Step 1. Encourage the visitors to speak as though they are the host of that land as this helps really promote enhanced understanding and a 'felt' experience of that land.
- Invite visitors to ask any clarifying questions to the land owner.
- When the visit is over, ask everyone to return to their land.
- Repeat this process until everyone has visited and developed their understanding across all of the lands.

3. **Co-creating Our Land**
- Ask the team members to get a fresh flipchart on which to create their collective land and to place this in the middle of the room. (At this stage you may like to have some pens available for the team to write the principles of Our Land.)
- Hold the space for a brainstorming session on what aspects of each other's lands they want to bring to their collective land. (Team members can import aspects from other people's lands, but not from their own!) "What would each of you like to import from the others' lands?"
- Encourage individuals to take turns to add to the vision for the combined land, helping them stress-test ideas and build something that everyone feels they can (1) support and (2) occupy.
- Check if there is anything else the team would like to add – "Is there anything else that needs to be included in Our Land for it to meet your needs?"
- Once the necessary discussion has taken place, and inevitable compromises have been made, ask the team, "What is available to us from here in our new land?"

Reference

Rød, A., and Fridjhon, M. (2016) *Creating Intelligent Teams: Leading with Relationship Systems Intelligence*. Randburg: KR Publishing.

Jackie Gittins, **Francesca King** and **Layla Coe** are qualified team coaching practitioners at Coach Nudge.

Sweet Spot Identifier (Career)

Ingredients

Flipchart and pens or

Paper and pens

Description

The Sweet Spot Identifier is based on a Venn diagram with three circles: passions and interests; strengths and skills; market value. By helping a client populate each circle with their own thoughts, they can begin to think about where there is overlap. It is this overlap that represents the sweet spot where an item meets all three criteria: passions, skills and what the market wants/needs.

When does it work best?

It can be overwhelming for clients to work out what they want to do when either changing jobs or starting a new business. Often clients look to others or to their coach to suggest or even tell them what they should do. This exercise helps a client to start with self-reflection, not outside direction, and prompts them to start answering the questions they have about "What next?" The identification of the intersection allows them to move forward in their professional endeavours, with more control over where they are heading and why. It can serve as a really accessible way of prompting a client to be curious to explore their strengths and values as they see them, before then also looking for external inputs to develop their thinking.

Step by step

1. Introduce the diagram by drawing the three circles with the client.
2. Ask the client to think about the following:
   a. What are your passions and interests?
   Expand this with questions around values, vision and goals, and passions: What do they care about? What energises rather than drains

them? What do they spend money on? What do they enjoy doing or learning about? When they're not working, what do they spend time on? Is there a problem they have or can see that they would like to solve? Is there something they see in society that they'd enjoy improving?

Help them to understand that these are all clues about what they deeply care about. Discuss the concept that, when we work on something we genuinely care about, we're much more likely to invest the time and effort it takes to become successful.

Ask them to note or plot these on the Venn diagram in the appropriate section. Then explore the next question:

b. What are your strengths and skills?

Ask your client to think about what they are good at and what skills come easily. What do others say they're good at and why? Are they a people person or do they prefer to work in isolation? What skills have they leant on up to now and what has this meant for their results? (For example, writing, speaking, organising, public speaking, editing, managing, collaborating.) When they work with people, is their role generally helper, leader, motivator, listener, negotiator or trusted advisor? Are they mostly technical or creative, efficient, outgoing, a detail person, a people person, and so on?

Suggest to them that they are probably good at several things and ask them to consider what they enjoy most and what they want to improve on. Help your client to steer away from job titles or genres and to be as basic as they can be, breaking things down as far as they can.

Again, ask them to place these on the Venn diagram in the appropriate section. Then explore the next question:

c. What is your market value?

Who is likely to pay for the things listed in (a) and (b), skills and strengths and passions? Which people or organisation types would benefit from what they have to offer? Who do they want to help? Would acquiring other skills or experience make them more marketable – and if so, which?

This type of self-assessment can start to help them to define the best possible job opportunities for them to pursue.

3. Take time to explore a client's other needs – their overall work environment, sitting at a desk, moving around, uninterrupted time, predictable, variety, interaction with others, solo, what kind of inter-action (adult, child, group, etc.) and so on.

4. Ask the client to reflect on the diagram, and then ask how they feel about what is represented in the overlap area. Does it highlight any specific opportunities they could look further into? Does it reinforce any of the ideas they've had? What surprises are there (if any)?

5. Conclude by inviting the client to consider what actions they could take to progress towards this sweet spot and exploring what obstacles may need to be removed or worked around to turn these ideas into reality.

Maggie Grieve is an accredited leadership and team development coach, consultant and facilitator with 30 years of working with organisations and leaders across the world. She owns her own business, Ping Thinking, and is an external coach for NHS England.

The PERMA Wheel

Ingredients

PERMA Wheel image printed out or available to share online

Paper, pens, coloured pencils

When does it work best?

The tool works best for clients who like a scientific or evidence-based approach, including psycho-education. It also works well for clients who are visual learners. It is of obvious use in coaching for wellbeing, work–life balance and resilience, but recent research has also linked the elements of PERMA with performance at work (Donaldson et al., 2022), so it is not simply a tool to sit in the wellbeing space.

Description

The PERMA Wheel is a positive psychology coaching technique based on the PERMA framework for wellbeing, which was developed by Martin Seligman (2011) as part of his Wellbeing Theory (WBT). PERMA sets out the five main factors that are the building blocks of human flourishing. They are:

- **Positive emotion** – having moments in life where we experience emotions such as love, joy, happiness and excitement
- **Engagement** – experiencing 'flow', or a sense of being immersed and absorbed in an activity
- **Relationships** – being connected to and being valued by others in positive, mutually beneficial relationships
- **Meaning** – being connected to a higher purpose or something greater than oneself
- **Accomplishments** – feeling a sense of achievement and pride in the things that one does.

PERMA's strength is its evidence base. Studies have found positive associations between the five elements and wellbeing, health, happiness and job satisfaction (de Carvalho et al., 2021).

PERMA can also be used with the concept of evidence-based 'positive psychology interventions' or PPIs. These are things that are known to build wellbeing and fall under the categories of: savouring, gratitude, kindness, empathy, optimism, strength-building and meaning-orienting (Parks and Layous, 2016). They could include: mindfulness, gratitude journalling, finding ways to strengthen connection with others or simply goal-setting.

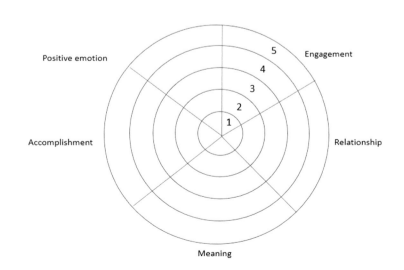

The PERMA Wheel

Step by step

1. Introduce the concept of PERMA and talk the client through the five elements. Ask, "What does [each element] mean for you in terms of your goal/the conversation we've been having?"
2. Show your client how to draw out or fill in the wheel, scoring themselves in relation to how far they feel each element is showing up for them at the moment, on a scale of 1–10, where 1 is low and 10 is high. Invite them to colour in or shade the segments. Ask them to "Tell me more about why you've given [each element] that score" and "How do you feel about that?"
3. Invite them to score where they would like to be, and either colour in the gap in a different colour or leave it unshaded. Ask, "What would it mean for you to increase the part [this element] plays in your life?", "What would it give you if you could increase your score in this area?" or "What would you be seeing/hearing/thinking/doing if you were able to be more in the X space?"
4. Either introduce the concept of positive psychology interventions (PPIs) by telling them that there are evidence-based things they can do to boost their wellbeing in these areas, asking them, "Which of these interventions would you like to think about in more detail?" and helping them to plan some actions, or…
5. Ask them, "What sort of things would help you build more of X into your life?" or "What is within your control to move forward right now?" They can then come up with their own ideas.
6. Encourage meta-cognition by inviting the client to take a step back and reflect on the conversation. Ask, "What insights are starting to emerge for you?"
7. To encourage them to take action, invite them to draw up a plan. Ask them, "Where would you like to start?" and "What is your next step after this?"

References

de Carvalho, T.F., de Aquino, S.D., and Natividade, J.C. (2021) Flourishing in the Brazilian Context: Evidence of the Validity of the PERMA-profiler Scale. *Current Psychology*, 42: 1,828–1,840.

Donaldson S.I. et al. (2022) PERMA+4: A Framework for Work-Related Wellbeing. Performance and Positive Organizational Psychology 2.0. *Frontiers in Psychology*, 12. Available from: https://doi.org/10.3389/fpsyg.2021.817244.

Parks, A.C., and Layous, K. (2016) Positive Psychological Interventions. In J.C. Norcross et al. (eds), *APA Handbook of Clinical Psychology: Applications and Methods*, pp.439–449. American Psychological Association.

Seligman, M. (2011) *Flourish: A New Understanding of Happiness and Wellbeing and How to Achieve Them*. London: Nicholas Brearley Publishing.

Catherine Wilton is a coach, supervisor and leadership development specialist with over 20 years' experience of supporting individuals and groups. She is Programme Director of the NHS Leadership for Personalised Care programme and Collaborative Leadership Academy.

The WOOP Framework

Ingredients

None

When does it work best?

WOOP works best as part of the main goal-setting discussion during coaching and is useful for both personal and professional goals. It can strengthen and complement the GROW model, for those using that in their coaching.

Description

Many of us, when setting goals, have been encouraged to focus on positive visualisation – thinking of the ideal future we want. However, the downside of positive visualisation may mean we become complacent, putting less effort in because we already have a sense of achievement. Mental contrasting, however, is the act of positive visualisation of achieving a goal combined with visualising the internal struggle that could impede achieving that goal.

Thinking about potential obstacles and planning for how we'll overcome these obstacles are the steps we can often miss out. Professor of psychology Gabriele Oettingen has developed an evidence-based framework underpinned by the concept of mental contrasting. The framework, referred to as WOOP, helps people to ground their dreams in reality and mobilises dreams as a tool for taking direct action. WOOP stands for:

- **W**ish
- **O**utcome
- **O**bstacle
- **P**lan.

Step by step

Make sure the client is somewhere they can think and imagine. As WOOP draws on imagery, it's important to create the space for their imagination to be free. Give the client following instructions:

1. Think about a **wish** they want to achieve in the next three months (they can change the timeframe to suit their needs).
2. Imagine that wish in detail. It should be challenging, fulfilling but realistic.
3. Summarise their wish in three-to-six words.
4. Now let their thoughts and feelings run free. Imagine what it would feel like to achieve the best **outcome** of their wish.
5. Think about what the best result will be from achieving their wish. How will they feel? Imagine and then vividly describe the outcome.
6. Summarise the outcome in three-to-six words.
7. Now, think about the **obstacles** inside them – the things that might hold them back.
8. Think about their behaviours and thoughts that could hinder them. Vividly describe them in detail.
9. Now choose one main inner obstacle that might prevent them achieving their wish.
10. Summarise that obstacle in three-to-six words.

11. Thinking about their main obstacle, what **plan** can they put in place to overcome that obstacle?
12. Come up with ideas for actions they could take and thoughts they could think.
13. Choose an effective action or effective thought that can help them overcome the main obstacle.
14. Create an 'if–then' plan. Complete the statement:
    "If [insert main obstacle], then I will [insert action]."

Dr Hayley Lewis is a chartered psychologist and registered occupational psychologist.

Three-way Peer Supervision

Ingredients

None

Description

This tool consists of three coaches coming together and giving each other the space to be coached, to be mentored, to gain an external perspective or to practise coaching in a safe environment.

When does it work best?

This is useful all along the coach's professional journey. It can be performed with the same colleagues on a periodic basis or with different networks of colleagues.

Step by step

1. Set ground rules. These may include details around starting and ending on time, confidentiality (what is discussed in the room, stays in the room), respect for others' experiences, amount of challenge and support, and so forth.
2. Take alternate turns, each selecting which option you want to embark on that day: being coached, being mentored, gaining an external perspective or practising coaching in a safe environment (each described below respectively).

Coach	Coaching and/or mentoring	Get perspectives
Once a member chooses to coach, another member volunteers as a client and the third plays the observer role. The coaching takes place as it would in a regular session. Once finished, the observer asks the 'client' for their thoughts, then asks the same of the 'coach', and finally the observer shares their observations.	Once a member chooses to be coached/mentored, another person volunteers to coach, and the third plays the observer role. The coaching takes place as it would in a regular session. Once finished, the observer asks the coach who acted as 'client' for their thoughts, then they ask the 'coach' for their thoughts, and finally the observer shares their observations.	Once a member asks for perspectives, that person shares their issue or dilemma, and thinks out loud for about 10 minutes. This is followed by a question they would like answered. The peer supervisors ask clarification questions or coaching style questions, then they speak from their experience or something that came up for them: an object in their room, a metaphor, a song, a poem, a quote, information, others. Finally, closing thoughts are shared and the session moves on.

Three-way Peer Supervision

The group will alternate the following roles:
- Supervisee (the one choosing the activity)
- Peer supervisor (the one supporting the supervisee)
- Peer supervisors and time keeper (the one supporting the supervisee and keeping time).

This also works well as a walking session, if the participants like outdoor coaching.

Claudia Day is a coach and entrepreneur, co-founder of My Coaching Place, part of the AC UK leadership team, and holds a master's in coaching and behavioural change (Henley) and a master's in business administration (MIT).

Self-soothing

Ingredients

Pens

Paper/ Worksheet
(see table below)

**When does it
work best?**

The tool works
best for clients
experiencing high
levels of stress or
during periods of
heightened anxiety
or distress.

Description

Our five senses – sight, hearing, taste, smell and touch – can be effective routes
to help us reach states of greater relaxation and peace. For periods of emotional
distress, drawing on these five senses can help as pathways to lowering stress
sensations and pressure, and thus contributing towards greater wellbeing.

Step by step

1. The coach can invite the client to work through each of the five senses to
   identify actions they can take using each of the senses. Different people
   enjoy different sensations more than others, and different tastes or
   smells. The goal of these activities is to help the client to reach a state of
   relaxation, where they are more able to think and behave more effectively, in a more relaxed and controlled state.
2. The coach might, for example, create a worksheet with tables for each of
   the options and invite the client to review the worksheet and select their
   favourite options.
3. Discuss their choices and invite the client to test out one when emotions
   are triggered, and make a note of how this felt.
4. In the next session, review how the client has progressed.
5. With the client, identify four-to-eight different strategies that work best
   for them.

Table: Self-soothing Worksheet

Sense	Options	Choices
Sight	1. Go to the countryside or a park and enjoy the trees or a lake 2. Go to the seashore and enjoy the sand and waves 3. Find pictures on the internet of your favourite place 4. Go to a gallery and enjoy art 5. Watch a favourite movie 6. Start a collection of pleasurable pictures and look at them when needed	

Self-soothing

Hear	1. Talk to a person that you like and whose voice makes you happy 2. Listen to your favourite music 3. Go to a park, river or beach nearby and listen to the sound of birds, wind and water 4. Sing your favourite song in the shower 5. Listen to an audio book	
Smell	1. Put on a favourite perfume or cologne 2. Light a scented candle 3. Cook a meal that smells delicious 4. Pick fragrant flowers, such as roses, from your garden 5. Go to a bakery or coffee shop and breath in	
Taste	1. Cook a favourite meal and savour its taste 2. Go to a favourite restaurant 3. Eat comfort food such as chocolate, ice cream or crisps 4. Drink coffee, tea or cocoa and savour the taste 5. Eat a fresh piece of fruit, such as mango or apples 6. Chew a stick of gum	
Touch	1. Wrap yourself in a soft blanket 2. Stroke a dog or cat 3. Take a cold shower or a hot bubble bath 4. Get a massage 5. Cuddle a favourite teddy bear	

Jonathan Passmore is a chartered psychologist, accredited master coach, team coach, supervisor, author and professor at Henley Business School.

Time Perspective

Ingredients

Online Time Perspective Inventory

When does it work best?

This tool works best with any client who appears to be too focused on one time perspective. This can show up in various ways. For example, a client who describes a fear of failing, having experienced a difficult situation in the past, and who dwells on what could go wrong could be high in past–negative or present–fatalistic. The client who is too focused on immediate urgent tasks while ignoring longer-term and important projects may find their score for present–hedonistic is high. A future-oriented client may describe burnout and a lack of work–life balance or a preoccupation with career progression.

Description

We each have our own particular relationship to time. The way that we view time can have a significant impact on how we choose to spend this limited resource and can influence our success at work, our health, and psychological and mental wellbeing. Time Perspective is a tool that helps a client to understand their attitude to time. It facilitates a conversation about making the best use of the hours available to us and shifting towards a balanced time perspective for greater wellbeing and happiness. Based on many years of research, Philip Zimbardo and John Boyd describe the six most common time perspectives in the Western world (Zimbardo and Boyd, 2008), five of which are used in the Time Perspective Inventory. These are:

Past–positive – having a positive attitude towards your past experiences, be they good or bad. This can result in being cautious, which may be limiting.

Past–negative – viewing past experiences from a negative standpoint. This can lead to feeling resentful and a sense of regret.

Present–hedonistic – living for the moment, short-term gratification and immediate rewards. This is process focused rather than outcome focused. It can bring about the taking of greater risks as well as a lack of planning for the future.

Present–fatalistic – resigned to feelings of discontentment with the present; belief that lives are externally controlled. This perspective can lead people not to acknowledge their contributions towards their own success but to take the blame for failures. It can result in feeling anxious and depressed.

Future – weighs up current actions with an eye towards future outcomes. This can be highly goal-focused but relationships and work–life balance may take a back seat to ambitions.

The online Time Perspective Inventory has 61 questions and provides the client with their scores for each time perspective, based on the answers they submitted to the questionnaire. The client can compare their scores to the 'ideal' time perspective suggested by Zimbardo and Boyd. They can also determine how close to the average they are, measured against other respondents, including a significant US sample. The client can also determine if any of their scores are in the top or bottom percentiles. A coaching conversation can focus on what aspects of the client's time perspective piqued their curiosity, helping them to become more aware of how their time perspective is manifesting in their life.

Time Perspective

Step by step

1. Describe the concept of Time Perspective and its potential impact on our behaviours.
2. Ask if the client is interested in understanding how their own perspective on time may be influencing their decisions or limiting them in unexpected ways.
3. Provide the link to the Time Perspective Inventory (listed below) and ask that they complete it before the next session.
4. Review together, initially by asking, "What strikes you about your time perspective?"
5. This then leads to a conversation about how their time perspective is playing out in their work and personal lives, followed by ideas and actions that the client comes up with to shift towards a balanced time perspective.
6. The conversation may also identify how the client's time perspective is at odds with the organisational environment and expectations in which they work.

Reference

Zimbardo, P., and Boyd, J. (2008) *The Time Paradox: The New Psychology of Time that Will Change Your Life*. New York, NY: Free Press.

The Time Perspective Inventory can be found at: https://www.thetime-paradox.com/zimbardo-time-perspective-inventory/.

Sarah Gledhill is an accredited coach who specialises in the higher education and non-profit sectors, following an international fundraising career.

Using the Meaning Centred Coaching Model to Power Transformational Coaching

Ingredients

Meaning Centred
Coaching model
diagram

A4 paper

Pencils/pens

Description

Meaning matters to almost everyone. Most people desire to live a life that is meaning-full. The Meaning Centred Coaching model (MCC) provides an approach to developing a client's relationship to meaning on an ongoing basis. The model encompasses a holistic approach that considers the impact of meaning on the domains shown in the model graphic below .

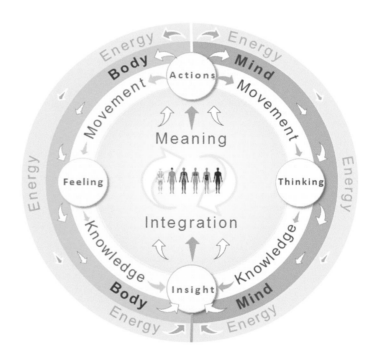

When does it work best?

This tool is particularly useful when introduced shortly after you have started working with a new client. It serves to familiarise the coach with what the client experiences as meaningful and acts as a guide for the energy of the coaching, no matter what the topics are from session to session.

The model is best rolled out with the client over a few sessions. The four main fields of the model – meaning, movement, knowledge and integration – can be seen as areas to visit in a variety of sequences over time. The client will quickly become familiar with them.

Step by step

1. *Session 1*: With their consent, introduce the subject of meaning to your client by asking what matters most to them. This can be on several scales. Questions might include: "What seems to matter today?", "What seems to matter in your whole life?" and "What has mattered to you in the past that still matters to you today?" Answers to these types of questions can vary. Some may be practical – for example, a client may say "What matters most is getting promoted". This is a statement of an action that they desire to take place and is not necessarily meaning-full. Often, clients will report things as mattering to them that are driven by some kind of fear-avoidance wish or ego fulfilment. This is not of course wrong, but the coach needs to stay aware of the different ways that people interpret meaning. For the purposes of the model, what the coach is seeking to encourage is the revealing of what the client wishes to experience and be in relationship to at their deepest level. Examples might range from family, to wishing to resolve some deep human or social issue, to heal themselves or others, to become wealthy and so on. It is important to remember that meaning can be very different for people and what they feel is meaningful at any given time is not necessarily in alignment with other people's values – including the coach's!

2. Experiment with different kinds of questions, such as: "What might you change if you had the power and resources to change anything?" As you move deeper into the conversation, expect to hear values, both core and general. Some people are easily clear about what has the most meaning to them; other people can be confused and the process painful. It can be the case that some people cannot articulate what matters most to them, as they hold a belief that what they yearn for is impossible to achieve. This can be connected to grief and anger.

3. As you proceed through this exploration of meaning, listen and watch out for energy shifts. Meaning is usually a vital, alive thing that manifests in energy. This energy is discernible in the way a person speaks, moves and expresses themselves. Use coaching skills of reflecting, questioning and clarifying to distil the meanings into coherent phrases or items. Work towards a temporary shortlist.

4. Towards the end of the session, ask the client to hone down the meaning-full items to a list by order of importance, at this point in the conversation. If there are a few that are all important, acknowledge that and then ask them to choose one, for now, that you can build an enquiry around as a coaching assignment.

5. Close the session by asking: "To stay connected to this [insert the client's meaning-full item here] what do you feel has to happen?"; "What are some of the things that you can and might do to bring this meaning more centrally, more closely and more deeply into your life?"

6. *Session 2*: This next session, we move into the Movement field of the MCC model. Connection to meaning releases energy and energy is active. Energy wants to move, transmit, transform. It is felt and visible. When clients are connected to meaning, they want to *do* things – set up

companies, talk to people, make plans to transform things that they feel need and can be transformed. The assignment you set at the end of the previous session was about that.

7. This session is about unpacking and exploring what the world of movement is for the client in their experience of the things that matter most to them, their meanings.

8. Coach them to make some sense and clarity about what they want to do. Coach them to come to a plan of action. In this session, be sure to keep focused on what the meaning is that they are planning around. Be mindful that they may try to jump into too much action and that managing the energy is important. As the model shows, place equal emphasis in your questioning on thinking processes and feelings.

9. At the close of the session create a coaching agreement about specifically what they are going to do in between sessions and build in accountability.

10. *Session 3*: Knowledge and Integration. In this session the client will have completed some, or all, of the assignments they agreed to. And they will have learned something about themselves and what they are trying to do. That learning is important. Watch out for a slump. Sometimes the energy can burn brightly and then dim somewhat as the effort of practical application and task completion becomes a reality. Perhaps someone who is key in their lives did not respond in expected ways. Perhaps others were not as excited about the project of the person enhancing their own life towards living more meaningfully. Whatever arises needs to be reviewed by the client. Coach the client to create a clear summary of key learnings. Then move to the integration stage. Ask: "What are you going to do with this new learning, the information you have?"; "Where does it fit in your approach to your next steps?"; "What adjustments might you make in view of what you now know?"; "Do you need to step back from certain people? Or cement new relationships? Rethink a career plan from scratch? Or move to a different track?"; and "How is your learning to be integrated?" Again, in the midst of this exploration, keep the touchstone of meaning close by and keep the client aware of it as they move through options. When stuck, which happens often, ask: "Which of these options are most likely to bring you closer to what is most meaningful?" Whilst there are no guarantees about any course of action or choice made, the client moving their lives forward because they are guided by meaning is the most likely way to bring fulfilment closer.

11. Close this session with agreed actions, enquiry or what seems appropriate as guided by the client. Return to this sequence as need.

Note: Image used with the permission of the author.

Anthony Eldridge-Rogers is a coach, facilitator, author and speaker specialising in Recovery and Wellness Coaching and the Meaning Centred Coaching model he created.

What Is Your Legacy?

Ingredients

Paper (to note responses on)

When does it work best?

The technique works best when a client is transitioning into a new role, or when they are working on moving from being results-oriented to being more purpose-focused.

Description

When starting out in a new role there is a lot to think about. Expectations around what needs to be delivered are usually high and can feel overwhelming. It may sound odd to start a new role by thinking about what you would like to leave behind when you move on! However, having clarity about your legacy can act as a lighthouse from the very start of your role. When tough decisions or change come along, your values can anchor you and your intended legacy can help steer you in the direction you want to head. This series of questions helps to focus the mind and energy on what is important and will bring a sense of purpose in the longer term.

Step by step

1. Open the coaching conversation by exploring what 'legacy' means to the client.
2. Explain the purpose of the exercise.
3. Ask the client to visualise their last day in this role. Perhaps they are reading the announcement about them leaving or listening to what people say as they raise a glass to them.
4. Use the following questions as a base from which to explore. Delve deeper into aspects with further questions and observations:
   - How would you like your team to remember you?
   - How would you like your colleagues/peers to remember you?
   - How would you like your customers/stakeholders to remember you?
   - How would you like your manager to remember you?
   - What would you like to pass on to the next generation at work?
   - What is one thing you would like to have achieved in three months' time? Six months? One year? Three years? Five years? (Notice what changes over the time periods.)
   - What is the first small step you can take now that will enable you to fulfil your legacy?
   - How will you know if you are fulfilling your legacy?
5. Close the exercise by exploring what the client has learned and would like to take forward.
6. It may be useful to share the article highlighted in the references after the session.

Reference

Sanyin, S. (2023) Ask Sanyin: How Can I Shape My Legacy as a Leader? *MIT Sloan Management Review* (15 February 2023).

Claire Finch is an accredited executive coach who supports individuals and teams to find and optimise their sources of energy to unlock their potential.

Three Wishes

Ingredients

Picture of a magic lamp

Post-it notes

Pen

Description

The image of a lamp or a genie is used to help the client become more creative in thinking about their goals or choices, where they may be bogged down by their existing view of the situation. The idea is to remove the current perceptions of what is and is not possible or realistic, so the client starts to set aside these preconceptions.

When does it work best?

This works well when a client is engaged in the coaching experience and wants to make change, but is finding it hard to identify positive goals (i.e. when they can only frame the situation as things they *don't* want to do or be any more). It also works well to help a client become more creative in their thought process as they identify potential options to explore.

This could also be used in a group or team scenario where there is a sense of mutual stuckness.

Step by step

1. Show your client the lamp/image. Ask them to imagine that the lamp also has a genie who has three wishes that she is offering the client in relation to their current situation. Allow enough time for the client to absorb this description of what's on offer. Someone who is stuck in more of a negative train of thought can find it harder to take on board the idea of the 'art of the possible'. You could ask them questions at this stage to ask how they feel about the existence of the genie to help them have that thinking time.
2. Once the concept is established, ask them what they would ask for. They may seek clarification – for example, asking "Can I ask for any wish or does it need to be realistic?" Reassure them that there are three wishes, and only three, and that these wishes should relate to the topic of the coaching conversation, but that they can be for anything.
3. Ask the client to note their chosen wishes down on Post-it notes. Then move on to the evaluation stage, as follows.
4. Ask them to look at their three Post-it notes and to consider each one in turn, and then all three together, evaluating two things:
   1. To what extent are some elements of each wish already in place?
   2. To what extent is it possible to plan some initial steps to move closer to at least one of the wishes.
5. Encourage your client, having considered Step 4, to identify what could be achieved and encourage them to think about what commitments they could make towards the overall topic now.

Reference

Van Niewerburgh, C. (2014) *An Introduction to Coaching Skills: A Practical Guide*. London: Sage.

Maggie Grieve is an accredited leadership and team development coach, consultant and facilitator with 30 years of working with organisations and leaders across the world. She owns her own business, Ping Thinking, and is an external coach for NHS England.

The Three Horizons Framework

Ingredients

Paper and pen

Picture of the Three Horizons Framework (helpful if using online)

Flipchart paper, pens and masking tape (if using with a group)

Description

The Three Horizons Framework is a tool to encourage reflection about change and how to achieve it. It enables an individual or team to consider challenges they are facing in the present, where they would like to be in the future and what they need to do now to ensure that new ways of working can emerge and take root.

The framework was developed by Bill Sharpe of International Futures Forum for the UK Foresight Programme. It consists of a graph with three lines, each representing a different version of the future. The x-axis represents time and the y-axis represents to what extent that perspective is 'business as usual' in terms of ways of working and thinking. Crucially, all perspectives are present at any one time, just at varying degrees.

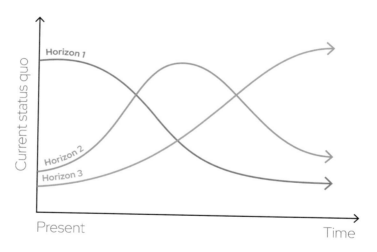

Diagram: The Three Horizons Framework

- **Horizon 1 (H1)** represents the current world view and the systems and infrastructure that support it. H1 ways of working might be outdated or no longer fit for purpose, even though they would have made sense at one time. You can think of this as the 'managerial' horizon.
- **Horizon 2 (H2)** is a transitional space of innovation, experimentation, tension, complexity and uncertainty. Some people will be trying out new things to bring H3 closer to reality. Other innovations might be overtly or inadvertently helping to preserve the status quo. You can think of this as the 'entrepreneurial' or 'disruptive' horizon.
- **Horizon 3 (H3)** represents a vision of the future and a completely new way of doing things. It feels very different to H1, and is rooted in values

and expressed as dreams and aspirations. You can often see glimpses of that future in the present. You can think of this as the 'visionary' horizon.

Many coaching clients are working in H2 – the zone of complexity and disruption – whether they like it or not. They might desire the H3 vision but not know how to get there. They might be experienced H1 leaders, but are being forced to change, to stay relevant as sands shift around them. H2 brings challenges too – it's not always possible simply to stop doing one thing and start doing something else. Health services can't suddenly stop spending money on treatments and spend it all on prevention of ill-heath instead, even if it is the right thing to do. Companies might need to invest in new technologies at the same time as keeping income coming in from old products. The framework is a useful tool to bring these perspectives into view, to identify both what is helpful and what is unhelpful, and guide next steps in leading change.

Step by step

1. Explain the model and draw it out or show the client a picture. If working with a group, use a wall-sized piece of paper (you can stick lots of flipchart sheets together with masking tape).
2. Get them to **describe H1**. Ask: "Where are we now?", "What are the key characteristics of business as usual?", "What brought us to this place?" and "Why is it not fit for purpose anymore?" If you are doing this one to one, you can get the client to write on the sheet as you go along. If you are working with a group, get participants to write their answers on Post-it notes and stick them along the H1 line on the left-hand side where H1 is dominant.
3. Then ask: "Is there anything we like or value about it that we would like to keep?" These reflections are placed on the right-hand side of the line, where H1 is less dominant.
4. Repeat the process by getting them to **describe H3**. Ask: "Where do we want to be/what's our future vision?", "What are the key characteristics of this vision?", "What would it look/feel/be like to be there?" and "What would people be saying if we were there already?" These reflections are placed on the right-hand side of the H3 line.
5. Then ask: "What values/history/knowledge is our vision based on?" and "What glimpses of that future can we see in the present?" These reflections are put on the left-hand side of the line where H1 is dominant. Moving along the H3 line, ask: "How could we harness these good ideas/innovations/new ways of working and spread them to more people/places?" and "Is anyone already doing it?"
6. Invite them to **describe H2**. Ask: "What is being disrupted as we move from H1 to H3?", "What systems/processes/structures/behaviours/world views are challenged?" and "What are people thinking/feeling about it?"

When does it work best?

Three Horizons works really well as part of a group process in which the framework is drawn out on a large sheet of paper so that lots of people can contribute insights and develop a collective understanding and plan of action. It can work equally well in one-to-one coaching for clients leading change in complexity and at times of transition. It has been used by companies to help think about and plan for the future, in terms of innovation and growth, and by organisations wanting to think about long-term social change or transformation.

7. Moving along H2 to the middle of the graph where H2 is dominant, ask: "What can we do now to harness the glimpses of the future that we see in the present?", "When we've done this before, how did we make it happen/how was it possible/who was involved?", "What kind of things should we now be doing or prioritising to take us to H3?", "What do we need to ask of others?", "What other new ideas do we have?" and "What do we need to put in place to ensure we don't get sucked back to Horizon 1?"

8. Give the client(s) space to reflect on what they have learned through the process and go away with some specific, actionable next steps.

Reference

Sharpe, B. (2020) *Three Horizons: The Patterning of Hope* (2nd edition). London: Triarchy Press.

Catherine Wilton is a coach, supervisor and leadership development specialist with over 20 years' experience of supporting individuals and groups. She is Director of the NHS Leadership for Personalised Care programme and Collaborative Leadership Academy.

Using Photography to Enhance Meaning in Life

Ingredients

Smartphone camera

Printer (optional)

Description

Having something to live for – in other words, a purpose in life – is one of the essential human needs. Therefore, one of the main aims of many coaching and psychotherapeutic approaches is to help clients live more meaningful and authentic lives aligned with their identities and values. To achieve this, we need to provide a context to explore clients' meaning in life – "the sense they make to their existence and the overarching life purpose they pursue" (Steger et al., 2014).

Finding meaning in life can feel like a challenging and elusive task. Therefore, coaches may use a range of established tools for assisting their clients' reflection, such as the Ikigai or the Wheel of Life (used both for finding meaning in life and goal setting) and validated questionnaires like the Purpose in Life (PIL) test (Crumbaugh, 1968) or the Life Regard Index (LRI) (Debats, 1998). They can also bring the topic into coaching conversations. However, articulating what life means can be a difficult task for some clients and the use of pictures representing instances of connection to others, to nature, to work or to creative moments can facilitate the process. This tool is inspired by Steger and colleagues (2014) and aims to help the client focus on those meaningful things and connect them with their meaning in life.

When does it work best?

Many clients know that they want to live meaningful lives, but they rarely stop to ask why they need meaning, how meaning affects them, or what really gives meaning and purpose to their own lives. This tool is effective in helping clients to take a pause and consider what makes their lives worth living and to what extent they are directed and motivated by valued life goals. Although the tool can be used at any point during the coaching assignment, it can be better placed after the first or second session. It can also be helpful after a significant (positive or negative) life experience.

Step by step

1. Invite your client to spend some minutes each day, for one week, taking pictures of things or representations of things that are important to them and that make their lives feel meaningful. These may include places, objects, people, pets, landscapes and such like. Ideally, they should take seven-to-ten pictures.

2. By the end of the week, the client will spend some time looking at and reflecting on each picture. As Steger suggested, the client will write down the answers to this question: "What does this photo represent and why is it meaningful?"
3. Invite the client to bring the photographs to the coaching session. Let them talk about all or some of them and explain what they represent and why they are meaningful. Then, as in any other coaching conversation, you will listen, reflect back and ask questions to help the client understand their reflection and connect the insights to their values, vision and goals.

References

Crumbaugh, J.C. (1968) Cross-validation of Purpose-in-life Test Based on Frankl's Concepts. *Journal of Individual Psychology*, 24(1): 74.

Debats, D.L. (1998) Measurement of Personal Meaning: The Psychometric Properties of the Life Regard Index. In P.T.P. Wong and P.S. Fry (eds), *The Human Quest for Meaning: A Handbook of Psychological Research and Clinical Applications*, pp.237–259. Lawrence Erlbaum Associates Publishers.

Steger, M.F., Shim, Y., Barenz, J., and Shin, J.Y. (2014) Through the Windows of the Soul: A Pilot Study using Photography to Enhance Meaning in Life. *Journal of Contextual Behavioral Science*, 3(1): 27–30.

Andrea Giraldez-Hayes is a chartered psychologist, accredited coach and supervisor. She is director of the MSc in Applied Positive Psychology and Coaching Psychology at the University of East London.

The *Telos* of Occupation

Ingredients

Pen and paper

When does it work best?

This works well for people who work in a profession or occupation that they consider to have a moral purpose. It can be useful for people who identify as a successful professional but who, because of promotion into a managerial role, personal ambition or the pressures of institutional demands, have lost connection with why they practise their profession.

Description

The virtue framework is based on Aristotle's philosophy. Unlike other ethical frameworks, it concentrates on the character of the individual, rather than their actions. Put simply, it argues that people who have developed a virtuous character will strive to do the right thing.

Recently, this approach has been applied to professions and other occupations. There are several key aspects to this, one of which is to understand what the moral purpose (*telos*) of the profession is. This is the ultimate end, the purpose for which there is no answer to the question "Why?" For example, the ultimate end of doctors is not to perform an operation or even to cure disease (as one can still legitimately ask "Why is that important?") but "to help people flourish by enabling them to optimise their health".

An understanding of the *telos* should describe the good that comes from the practice of the profession, as well as what makes it practically successful. A good doctor, who achieves their *telos*, will be both morally and practically good.

An explicit understanding of the *telos* also helps reflection about how best to practise one's occupation. Thus the description of medical *telos* given below opens up helpful conversations about who the 'people' are, what 'flourishing' and 'health' mean, and how what they are doing helps achieve these.

Finally, this exercise can help connect people back to internal goods that are obtained by the skilful practice of an occupation or profession. These internal goods are in contrast to external goods such as fame, fortune or reputation that can be obtained by doing other things. Often professionals have lost sight of why they decided to join their profession, and the joy that they get out of practising it, because their focus is exclusively on the external goods (often because of institutional pressures). An ability to recall the pleasure and fulfilment obtained from one's profession can be important in regaining motivation and balance in work.

Step by step

This can be the introduction to a number of sessions looking at the virtues that the client needs to be successful.

1. Discuss briefly the history of virtue ethics, how it unites practical and moral outcomes.
2. Give an example from a different profession/occupation to that of the client and show them how it can be used for reflection.
3. Ask them what they think the purpose of their profession or occupation is.

4. Accept their statement, but get them to dive deeper by asking them "Why?" or "What is the purpose of that?" You can ask why that purpose is good for their clients or for society. People will often start with a practical purpose (to do cardiac surgery) and move up a hierarchy of purposes (to mend the heart, to make people better, to give them health, to make them enjoy life…) until you reach a statement of which the question "Why?" cannot usefully be asked.

5. Write down the *telos* and explore its meaning. Be sure the wording is authentic for the client. Explore with them whether that would be recognised by other practitioners.

This can then become a resource for further explorations over the following weeks. These can include a reflection on their professional practice, a consideration of the internal goods that they obtain by their practice or the nature of the virtues that they could develop to achieve their *telos*.

References

George, A.J.T., and Rose, S. (2023) Ethical Decision-making: Virtues for Senior Leadership in Higher Education. *Management in Education*. Available from: doi.org/10.1177/08920206231172027.

George, A.J.T., Urch, C.E., and Cribb, A. (2023) A Virtuous Framework for Professional Reflection. *Future Healthcare Journal* (February 2023). Available from: doi.org/10.7861/fhj.2022-0121.

Andrew J.T. George is an executive coach who trained at Henley Business School, where he is now an honorary research fellow. He is Professor of Immunology at Imperial College London with a particular interest in research ethics and integrity and the nature of professions.

RESISTT

Ingredients

None

Description

RESISTT is a set of seven techniques drawn from DBT and, again, is useful for clients with overwhelming emotions. These feelings may be anger, but they can also be sadness. In clinical settings, this can lead to risk of self-harm or harm to others; in the workplace, it can often lead to a leadership style that others experience as 'toxic'.

When does it work best?

Like other DBT approaches, this tool works best with clients who are struggling to manage overwhelming emotions. As with all clients, the coach needs to be sensitive to clinical issues, and if they are concerned, they should refer clients to a medical doctor.

Step by step

1. The coach can start by explaining the approach to the client and the seven steps of the framework.
2. The coach invites the client to work through each of the seven steps and consider each as it applies to them and their situation.
3. The coach works to help the client develop a response for each of the seven steps, which the client can take away and practice.
4. In a follow-up meeting, the coach can invite the client to review their progress: what worked well, what less well, what could happen differently next time, which ones are worth repeating, which ones are worth replacing, which ones are worth excluding?

Table: RESISTT

Reframe	People can be trapped in 'black-and-white thinking': either everything is bad or everything is good. Reframing helps clients to move away from a black-and-white thinking style towards a more rainbow style of thinking based on evidence, recognising both good and less good aspects in their situation.
Engage in distraction	Distraction from a situation can help. Distractions can be long or short term. Long-term distractions can give us perspective, help us to recognise that this is not the only thing that is going on. Distractions such as helping in our community (altruistic acts) help us to see there is life beyond our immediate worries or current events. A second aspect is short term. This may take the form of a thinking experiment. For example, 'try to avoid thinking about a tiger' or engaging in a breathing exercise.
Someone else	Thinking about someone else (maybe someone we care about) and a pleasant time spent with them can help us during a situation that we are experiencing as stressful.

RESISTT

Intense sensations	Sensory stimulation can help. A cold shower, stepping outside without a coat on a cold day or holding an ice cube in our hand until it melts – all these can provide an alternative stimulation to help tackle rising, unhelpful emotions.
Shut it out	One option is to leave the situation. But for times when that's not possible (for example, presenting to a large group), an alternative is to place the rising emotions into a box: literally visualise a box and imagine placing the situation into it, closing the lid and putting it to one side.
Neutral thoughts	This involves placing oneself outside of the situation and into a neutral and calm environment. The client can be invited to close their eyes for 10 seconds (to others, it will simply look like they are thinking) and to think about themselves in a different place. Pleasurable, calm places like a wood, a lakeside or a gentle ocean can all work well. This can be accompanied by breathing in and out slowly to a count of 10 before returning to the situation.
Take a break	This step involves physically removing oneself from the situation for a few minutes. A comfort break can work well, providing a two- or three-minute opportunity to breathe and refocus before re-engaging.

Jonathan Passmore is a chartered psychologist, accredited master coach, team coach, supervisor, author and professor at Henley Business School.

Misfits

Ingredients

Misfits Game or
Kwirkeez

When does it work best?

The standard question to offer is "What kind of coach/supervisor/mentor/leader misfit are you?" This can be done quickly (as an introduction) or more deeply (looking at articulating your professional style) and it can be repeated (revisit the 'default' misfit with a particular client in mind).

Description

Misfits is a twist on a vintage card game for children. It offers a playful way of exploring our professional persona (for example, coach, supervisor, mentor or leader). Each misfit comprises five pieces: a hat, a face, a body and two legs; there are twelve different characters in the set. The invitation is to notice which pieces help you say something about how you work and then to create a misfit (typically choosing pieces from different characters, rather than selecting a whole original character).

Step by step

Give the client the following instructions

1. Familiarise yourself with the pieces by emptying the box and organising the cards into the twelve characters.
2. Pose a question appropriate to the work in hand – for example:
   • What kind of [leader, team member, coach] misfit are you?
   • What kind of misfit are you on a good day? And on a bad day?
   • When you were with this client, what kind of misfit did you become?
   • Which parts of your misfit feel established and which pieces do you feel are still evolving?
3. Narrate the story of which pieces you were attracted to and what they may symbolise for you. If you are listening to a person's narrative, offer questions that will encourage more storytelling rather than giving them your interpretation of their pieces.
4. Consider – which pieces came quickly, which pieces took longer to connect to? What might that tell you?
5. Consider – how did you build your misfit? Logically, spontaneously, hesitantly, swiftly? What might that say about your response to the posed question?
6. Find a way of capturing your misfit. From a developmental perspective, it can be helpful to revisit the misfit with a different question in mind.

Note: The characters of the original Misfits game reflect the time the game was developed; since then, language has changed. An updated set of characters, 'Kwirkeez', have been developed by Lucas and Sanbar (2023) and are available on a digital platform.

References

Lucas, M. (2020) *101 Coaching Supervision Techniques, Approaches, Enquiries and Experiments*, pp.68–70. Abingdon: Maidenhead.

Lucas, M., and Sanbar, P. (2023) Building Your Ideal Self? Try Kwirkeez. *Coaching Perspectives*, January 2023 (36): 46–47.

Michelle Lucas is an accredited executive master coach and an accredited master coach supervisor.

Categorisation index: using the tools in different coaching situations

The tools in this book cover a diverse range of topics and can be used in a wide range of coaching situations. We have put together a simple index of tools that you might find useful to support clients with certain presenting topics.

These categories are by no means exhaustive and the allocation of different tools to different categories is based purely on our editorial judgement. However, if you are stuck for inspiration or would like to explore a range of approaches for supporting clients with particular issues then this index may be helpful for you.